Editorial adviser Professor Asa Briggs
Editor Elizabeth Gundrey

THEN
1848

CONTENTS

The borders and typefaces used for headings in this issue were all popular in the 1840's when typography was marked by an exciting use of many different display faces.

The drawing on the cover is by Phiz, one of Dickens' illustrators, and shows a Chartist riot.

Newspapers were taxed, and bore this stamp to show the tax had been paid.

YEAR OF REVOLUTIONS

The year 1848 has passed down in history as the year of revolutions, with the "February days" in France ushering in a new phase in the struggles between the advocates of "movement" and the defenders of "order". Yet there were to be sharp reversals of fortune later in the year, particularly in France itself, where during "the June days" hope and comedy gave way to hate and tragedy. What remained throughout the year was a sense of drama, the drama both of political conflict and of the vulnerability of the human condition. Cholera spread relentlessly through Europe—from Asia—and across the Atlantic. Contemporaries considered it "a disease of society", noting that everywhere it travelled it frightened people and tested institutions. Only the frost of a new winter checked its advance.

Britain, which, to the surprise of the prophets of the 1840s, avoided revolution in 1848, could not avoid cholera. And one of the most important pieces of legislation carried through Parliament in 1848 was the first national Public Health Act. This act, controversial to the last, showed that the "condition of England" question was a central one in politics.

Yet if there was no revolution in Europe's most industrialized country, there was a great deal of discontent, particularly during the early months of the year. The same economic pressures which affected the European social and political balance had affected Britain also : indeed, it was Britain's financial and economic crisis in 1847 which had had repercussions throughout Europe. There was also fierce discontent across the Irish Sea, and people living in England, Scotland and Wales were aware throughout 1848 that Dublin as well as Paris was a city to watch.

In England itself there were disturbances almost every month until the autumn. The most dangerous of them took place after not before the widely reported Kennington Common affair of April and most of them were outside London in the troubled industrial areas. Nonetheless, Englishmen were beginning to draw what seemed to be the proper morals of the English story by April 1848. We were setting an example to Europe. The morals were summed up in the Annual Register for the year. "The dangerous assemblage was put down not by the troops, not by the public, but by the people themselves."

A SHAKE-UP OF CLASSES

It is necessary to consider the term "the people" more critically than the moralists did. There was a strong class sense in 1848. The "working classes" were divided, with some sections accepting the new industrial system and others rejecting it. There were also many survivals from an older social and economic structure. There were more shoemakers than coalminers, and one in ten of all females over nine years old was employed in domestic service. London itself was not an industrial city, though there were industries inside it.

While the Chartists were seeking, sometimes desperately, to mobilize full support, the "middle classes", a term used self-consciously and with pride in 1848, were placing their immense social weight behind the Constitution. Yet this did not mean that there was agreement about critical social relationships. One radical Member of Parliament called the working classes "helots of the land, having no concern with the laws except to obey them". Disraeli claimed, as he had done before, that it was only through the failure of "the gentry" that "a new profession has been discovered, the profession of agitation". A third independent-minded Member "upheld the middle classes against the gentry", the most common of the contradictory reactions of 1848. After Kennington Common, Lady Palmerston wrote to a friend giving "private details of our 'revolution', as the papers, though very full, could give only the public ones. Our terrace was divided into districts and all the servants made special constables." Her last sentence reads, "I am sure that it is fortunate that the whole thing has occurred, as it has shown the good spirit of our middle classes."

BRITANNIA'S RULE

If there was doubt about social relationships in 1848, there was also argument about Britain's position in the world. The repeal of the Navigation Acts produced a debate in Parliament which, though less bitter than the debate on the repeal of the corn laws in 1846, raised even more profound historic issues. Richard Cobden asked Parliament whether it was a good thing that they should always be singing Rule Britannia: "the constant assertion of maritime supremacy was calculated to provoke kindred passions in other nations". In reply

Disraeli, undoubtedly the wit of the year, said that while he would not sing Rule Britannia *for fear of distressing Mr. Cobden he was sure that the House would not encore* Yankee Doodle. *The President of the Board of Trade had described their times as " this age of commerce, peace, and internal improvement ": he, Disraeli, would describe it as " the age of no trade, of intended war, and of Communist bands tearing up railways ".*

Palmerston, the Foreign Secretary, was not one of the main speakers in this debate, but he made it clear where he stood on a different parliamentary occasion in 1848. In a year of revolutions Britain should be " the champion of justice and right " but not " the Quixote of the world ". Above all, British policy should protect British interests. " Our interests are eternal and perpetual, and those interests it is our duty to follow."

HAPPENINGS

Not all the drama of the year was associated with national or international conflict. There was an " unusual scene " at the consecration of the Bishop of Manchester in January when " a known vehement enemy of the bishop elect " stood forward and announced himself as " an opposer ": the following day there were troubles at Hereford where the new Bishop, the controversial Dr. Hampden, had so many ' opposers " that they took the case to the Court of Queen's Bench.

The most agreeable drama of the year was performed in May. In order to raise money for the purchase of Shakespeare's birthplace at Stratford, the second of two remarkable amateur performances of Tudor plays took place at the Haymarket Theatre. The Merry Wives of Windsor *had Mark Lemon, the editor of* Punch, *as Falstaff, George Cruikshank as one of his followers, G. H. Lewes as Sir Hugh Evans, Augustus Egg as Simple, and Charles Dickens as Justice Shallow. The merits of Dickens, in particular, were singled out by the critics. " The air of vacancy, the complacent chuckle, were sustained throughout with the greatest care." This was not the only complacent chuckle which was sustained in Britain throughout 1848.*

Asa Briggs

NOT SO *VERY* UNREASONABLE !!! EH?

John. "MY MISTRESS SAYS SHE HOPES YOU WON'T CALL A MEETING OF HER CREDITORS; BUT IF YOU WILL LEAVE YOUR BILL IN THE USUAL WAY, IT SHALL BE PROPERLY ATTENDED TO."

Punch

The Chartists deliver a Bill to Lord John Russell, Prime Minister.

THE CHARTIST CLIMAX

Working-class demonstrations were alarming in a year when all Europe was in ferment. When the Chartists—demanding manhood suffrage and other electoral reforms—organized meetings and marches, banks were sandbagged and Wellington marshalled his troops. But working men were too ill-educated and disorganized to achieve much.

The last big demonstration, on London's Kennington Common (10 April), fizzled out ; and, after many signatures on its monster petition to Parliament were shown to be crude forgeries, the Chartist movement gradually collapsed. Sporadic demonstrations in other parts of Britain ended only in arrests.

Government Proclamation

6 April.

Whereas the assemblage of large numbers of people, accompanied with circumstances tending to excite terror and alarm in the minds of her Majesty's subjects, is criminal and unlawful ;

And whereas not only those persons who take an active part in such assemblage, but those also who by their presence wilfully countenance it, are acting contrary to law, and are liable to punishment ; and whereas an Act of Parliament, passed in the 13th year of the reign of his late Majesty King Charles II, intituled " An Act against tumults and disorders, upon pretence of preparing or presenting public petitions or other addresses to his Majesty in the Parliament ", it was enacted that, that no person or persons whatsoever shall repair to his Majesty or both or either of the Houses of Parliament, upon pretence of presenting or delivering any petition, complaint, remonstrance, or declaration, or other addresses, accompanied with excessive numbers of people, nor at any one time with above the number of ten persons ;

And whereas a meeting has been called to assemble on Monday next, the 10th inst., at Kennington-common, and it is announced in the printed notices calling such meeting, that it is intended by certain persons to repair thence in procession to the House of Commons, accompanied with excessive numbers of people, upon pretence of presenting a petition to the Commons House of Parliament ; and whereas information has been received that persons have been advised to procure arms and weapons, with the purpose of carrying the same in such procession ; and whereas such proposed procession is calculated to excite terror and alarm in the minds of her Majesty's subjects ;

All persons are hereby cautioned and strictly enjoined not to attend, or take part in, or be present at, any such assemblage or procession.

And all well-disposed persons are hereby called upon and required to aid in enforcing the provisions of the law, and effectually to protect the public peace, and suppress any attempt at the disturbance thereof.

Public Offices Armed

Illustrated London News, 8 April.

Government is taking every precaution, in case there should be any manifestation of an outbreak among the working classes, who, it is stated, are to assemble on Monday next, on Kennington-common. A large supply of firearms and cutlasses have been sent from the Tower to the East India-house, and their different ware-houses, the Custom-house, Excise-office, the Post-office, Bank of England, the Mansion-house, the various departments at Somerset-house, the Ordnance-office, Pall-mall, the Admiralty, and the different Government offices at the West-end ; also to a great many of the banking-houses in the City, and the dock companies. The clerks and persons employed in these establishments will be ready to act, if absolutely necessary, against any outrage

Special Constable. "NOW MIND, YOU KNOW—IF I KILL YOU, IT'S NOTHING ; BUT IF YOU KILL ME, BY JINGO IT'S MURDER."

Punch

that may be committed by a mob. The swearing-in of special constables is proceeding rapidly in Lambeth, Walworth, Camberwell, the Borough, and the districts on the Surrey side of the water where the tradespeople and householders all show their desire to protect the public peace if called upon.

Feargus O'Connor, M.P., leader of the Chartists and editor of their paper, The Northern Star.

The Great Demonstration at Kennington

This is the Chartists' own account of what happened, in the newspaper controlled by O'Connor.

Northern Star, 15 April.

In the city upwards of 70,000 persons were sworn special constables.

The royal carriages and horses, and other valuables were removed from the palace. The whole of the Queen Dowager's carriages, horses, &c, were removed to Bushey.

The military force (exclusive of the artillery and Chelsea and enrolled out-pensioners) in and near London was as follows :— Royal horse guards ; 1st and 2nd life guards ; 12th lancers ; 7 battalions of foot guards ; 17th regiment of foot ; 62nd ditto ; 63rd ditto—making an available force of nearly 9,000 men.

Sandbagged Bank

At a very early hour hundreds were observed passing on to the immediate scene of the meeting, and hundreds were likewise to be observed at the different stations appointed to be most strictly attended to, attracted, no doubt, by the military arrangements, which to some were matters of curiosity, to others of alarm. The spectators of the Bank fortifications were very numerous through the day. A breastwork of sand bags, with loopholes for muskets and small guns, had been thrown up along the parapet wall of this establishment. In addition to this, at each corner of the building, musket batteries, bullet-proof, were raised, having loop-holes for small carronades. In the interior, in addition to the 900 clerks and servants sworn in as special constables, every one of whom was provided with a brace of pistols, a musket and a cutlass, there was a strong detachment of Foot Guards.

Apart from the innumerable special constables who assembled at the various wards, under the Aldermen, and the greater part of whom were provided with staves and armlets, upwards of 2,000 of the younger and more active specials were selected by the Aldermen and placed in direct communication with the City police.

At eleven o'clock the police and special constables marched in large bodies to the three bridges, and took up their station there in immediate communication with the metropolitan constables, who attended at each in great numbers. As, from previous communications, it was inferred that the Chartists would proceed with their petition from Kennington Common to the House of Commons over Blackfriars Bridge, that station was the point at which the most formidable resistance was contemplated.

Bridges Barred

It was generally believed in the City that the government had determined, at the latest Council, to offer no obstacle whatever to the assembling of the people at Kennington Common, or to their progress from thence with the petition to which ever bridge their movements might indicate their intention to pass over, but that it was resolved that every resistance should be offered to any greater number than ten of the petitioning body.

At Stepney Green a band of music, preceded by the flag of " The Stepney Society of Cordwainers," and attended by a large body of persons, made their appearance, and were there joined by vast numbers of the Chartists of that neighbourhood, bearing other banners with the inscriptions of " The People's Charter and No Surrender," " The Chartist Land Company of Whitechapel," &c. The procession then formed and defiled up the lane. Every court and alley contributed its quota to swell the numbers of the procession as it passed. The banners of the Irish party were the newest and handsomest.

The persons forming this procession seemed anxious to behave themselves in a most orderly manner ; no weapons of offence and not more than two or three walking sticks being perceptible. Not a single policeman or soldier was to be seen throughout the whole of the route. A number of women, wearing the tricolour, walked in the procession.

Caps of Liberty

Finsbury-square was the rallying point for the district of Finsbury.

The Sappers and Miners, at the Tower, were busily employed during the day in throwing sand bags upon that part of the fortress near the western entrance, and along the whole of the lower ramparts facing the river. The gates were kept closed throughout the day, and no person was allowed to enter except those who had business to transact within the fortress. Double sentries were also placed throughout the entire building.

At ten, sounds of music were found to proceed from a small band which marched into the square, followed by many thousands walking four abreast, the majority of whom were journeymen shoemakers. They bore no weapons of offence or defence. Scattered throughout the procession were men bearing small banners, on which were inscribed various devices and mottoes ; amongst the latter were, " The Charter and No Surrender,"

The gathering on Kennington Common

Illustrated London News

10

"The National Land Association," &c. There were also caps of liberty, fastened to the ends of bundles of twigs. The shopkeepers on this side of the water appeared to have great faith in the peaceable and orderly conduct of the procession, for, with the exception of two or three in Gracechurch-street, not a shop window was closed during the whole of their progress from Finsbury-square to London Bridge. By the time the procession reached Newington Causeway, the number of those who accompanied it on each side was as great as the procession itself. At twelve o'clock the procession reached the common, and mingled with the gatherings from the other districts of the metropolis.

Cavalry and Ordnance

The Knightsbridge Barracks were kept closed, but, on the occasional opening of the gates, it was perceived that they were crowded with troops. In Trafalgar-square it was that the police first appeared, and thence down to Palace-yard the body of the force were chiefly concentrated. Along the Strand, also, there were strong bodies of them with horse patrols ; and, as they kept constantly moving, and compelling the crowd to move, the streets were kept clear, and there was nothing that could be called a mob anywhere, although an immense number of persons were scattered about.

Each of the bridges was strongly defended by an immense mass of police and special constables, and at Westminster (down to which there was one uninterrupted array of police), there were upwards of 600, with a regiment of cavalry, and six pieces of ordnance ; added to which, there were, of course, the royal regiments, in barracks close at hand.

Silk Banners

At nine o'clock punctually the cordwainers were observed marching down Keppel-street, carrying banners and wearing rosettes. Shortly afterwards they were followed by the men of the Westminster district, many of them tailors and artisans. The spectators who now poured in from the New-road, Holborn, Tottenham-court road, and Gray's-inn-lane, almost filled the west side of the square, and rendered it a matter of some difficulty to pass through. At half-past nine o'clock loud cheers announced that the Irish Confederates had arrived. They marched down Montague-place, carrying orange and green banners, and many of them displaying temperance medals. The word having been given to fall in, the body was marshalled rank and file, and the people proceeded arm in arm, eight deep. The cordwainers took the lead, carrying a blue silk banner inscribed with the words "Liberty, Equality, and Fraternity. The Charter and No Surrender." Next came a flag-staff, surmounted with the cap of liberty, made of crimson cloth, with the motto "Divided we fall." The "Emmett Brigade" displayed a silk banner of crimson, white, and green, with the inscription, "What is Life without Liberty !" The banner of the Confederates was formed of green silk, fringed with orange. An ancient Irsh harp was emblazoned in gold, and underneath the words, "Let every man have his own country."

Kennington Common

We found every height, whence it was possible to obtain the most remote view, crowded to excess ; the windows of every house overlooking the common were crowded with elegantly dressed females, who appeared to be anxious spectators of the scene. Eleven o'clock had now arrived, and the processions from the various parts of town began to arrive. The first we observed was that of the Tower Hamlets, a magnificent *cortége*, comprising some 30,000 persons, and such was their conduct, peaceable demeanour and firmness, that a police inspector complimented them thereon. Next came the great western body, which started from Russell-square, a most magnificent body, amongst whom marched the body of shoemakers, the West End Men's [branch] alone exceeding 800 persons ; they were preceded by a banner, purchased by the apprentice lads in the trade, made of silk, inscribed, "Cordwainers, Liberty, Equality, Fraternity." The glorious bands of Irish Confederates and Repealers, who had turned out to exhibit their fraternisation with the English Chartists, had a splendid banner, a rich green silk one, with an orange border, surmounted with the harp of Erin, and inscribed, " Ireland for the Irish."

He then proceeded to state that preparations had been made for shooting from certain windows on the leaders of the movement. He was told this by Mr Alderman Humphrey in the House of Commons, and he had also received it from the police and others. He hoped there was firmness and resolution enough among them to act temperately, and not jeopardise their cause—for if they lost his (Mr O'Connor's) advocacy in the House of Commons, they might not easily obtain another one to take up his position. More than that, if they got into collision with the authorities, it would cause the Treason Bill to be passed that evening, without discussion, and the Charter would be lost for an indefinite time, if not for ever.

The meeting then broke up, and proceeded to form the Procession of Delegates.

About five minutes to ten, the Convention started from the hall, the procession being led by a car, drawn by four beautifully caparisoned horses, intended for the conveyance of the National Petition, profusely decorated with tri-coloured flags, of red, green, and white, and the inscriptions of " The Charter," " Universal Suffrage," " Annual Parliaments," " Vote by Ballot," " Equal Electoral Districts," " No Property Qualification," " Payment of Members," " We are Millions, and Demand our Rights," " Speak with the Voice—not with the Musket," &c., &c.

To this followed a second car, drawn by six horses, containing the principal members of the Convention, and the reporters of the press. They were loudly cheered by the people, who immediately fell into procession behind them, eight a-breast ; in addition to which vast numbers occupied the foot pavement on either side. The procession stopped for a few minutes at the offices of the National Land Association, to take up the National Petition, which consisted of five large rolls of paper of nine or ten feet in circumference each. The petition being lashed on to the car, the procession proceeded on its way.

At the Elephant and Castle a cheer was given, and from this point along the Kennington-road to the common the crowd presented the appearance of a moving mass of upwards of 10,000 persons. It proceeded in silence until the cars arrived within sight of the congregated thousands already assembled upon the common. The delegates were now surrounded by an enthusiastic crowd, and received with deafening and prolonged cheers, which Mr O'Connor and his brother delegates acknowledged by waving their hats. The assemblage was a grand and imposing sight, we heard the numbers variously estimated at from two hundred to five hundred thousand souls, from our experience of huge assemblies, we should say there could not be less than a quarter of a million persons present, on and around the common alone, whilst all the streets and avenues leading thereto were one dense mass of human beings.

O'Connor Speaks

Mr F. O'Connor, M.P., then came forward amid deafening cheers, which were taken up from those immediately around the car and re-echoed by the crowds in the outer circles over the whole common.

I have always contended [he said] for your rights, in and out of parliament, and to frighten me I have received at least 100 letters, telling me not to come here today, for that, if I did, my own life would be the sacrifice. My answer was this—" I would rather be stabbed to the heart than resign my proper place at the head of my children." (Shouts of " Bravo !") In yonder car (pointing to the vehicle which carried the Petition) go with you the voices of 5,700,000 of your countrymen. They, I, and the whole world, look to you for good and orderly and citizen-like conduct on this occasion. (Cheers.) As the Convention have received an intimation that the police will not let the procession pass the bridges, where they guard the ground, the Executive have decided that you shall not be brought into collison with an armed force. These cars will not be allowed to pass, the flags will not be allowed to be displayed. The Executive, therefore, will, as a deputation, take the petition. I will go to the house to remonstrate against this hinderance. I will present your petition, and I will make your voice heard

Lady's Newspaper.

O'Connor presents the monster petition.

throughout the length and breadth of the land. (Cheering.) I ask you, under these circumstances, through good and evil report, to stand by me to-day. (Cries of " We will.") Will you obey my counsel, and follow my advice? (" Yes, yes.") I will remain among you as a hostage, for, so help me God, I will not desert your cause until life deserts me. (Loud and prolonged cheering.)

About a quarter to two o'clock, (the delegates having previously separated,) three cabs were drawn up on the common, and the bales of the National Petition placed within and upon them, properly secured. The members of the Chartist Executive Committee accompanied the petition to the House of Commons, and the cabs drove off at a rapid pace, no attempt being made to follow them.

Police Provocation
Northern Star (reader's letter), 22 April.

Sir.—I take the liberty of sending you the copy of a letter the *Times* refused to insert, showing the partial manner they deal with matters likely to bring the enemies of the people into disrepute.

To the Editor of the *Times*

Sir.—I observe that you allow a person signing himself E.T.C. to express his satisfaction at the conduct of the police on Monday at Blackfriars Bridge ; permit me through the same medium, to express condemnation of the orders to stop the people from going over that bridge. I was one of those who joined the working people to assert the right of meeting to petition the legislature. The leaders having advised we should disperse on Kennington Common, I left with my friends to go home peacably, if I could, but in attempting to pass the bridge I was struck a violent blow with a bludgeon, although I produced my card which would prove I was on my direct way home. Knowing, as they did, the people did not intend coming back in procession, it appears to me they could have no other object in view but to excite the people to a collision. I am glad that the people did not retaliate, and I am certain that the excellent conduct of the working men, on that memorable day, has raised them fifty per cent in the estimation of the middle class. Trusting you will, in fairness publish this,

I am, sir, your obedient servant, M.P. Lee

A daguerreotype (early form of photograph) of the Duke of Wellington, who organised London's defence against the Chartists.

Public Grievance

Speech by Duke of Wellington in House of Lords,
11 April.

I do think that there is no rank of society should be allowed to suffer such a grievance as this metropolis has suffered within the last few days from the terror of this great meeting which has been called and which was to have consisted, it was said, of 200,000 persons. God knows how many thousands did attend, but still the effect was to place all the inhabitants of the metropolis under alarm, paralyzing all trade and business of every description, and driving individuals to seek for safety by arming themselves, for protection of the lives of themselves and of their neighbours, and for the security of their property. The inconveniences which were experienced this day have been now repeated for, I believe, a fourth time in this short session of Parliament. I trust that meetings may be limited to the numbers that can properly discuss them ; and that a great metropolis such as this is—the mart of trade and of credit—shall not be disturbed week after week by such transactions as have been going on around us for the last few days (cries of hear, hear, etc.).

Petition Discredited

Morning Chronicle (parliamentary report),
14 April.

Mr. Thornely brought up a special report from the select committee on public petitions, which was read by the clerk at the table as follows :— " The house, on the 26th of November last, directed your committee, in all cases, to set forth the number of signatures to each petition ; and also, having regard to the powers delegated to them, to report their opinion and observations thereupon. In the matter of signatures there has been, in their opinion, a gross abuse [loud cheers]. The honourable member for Nottingham stated, on presenting the petition, that 5,706,000 were attached to it ; but, upon the most careful examination the number of signatures has been ascertained to be 1,975,496 [loud and general cheers]. It is further evident to your committee, that on numerous consecutive sheets the signatures are in one and the same handwriting. Your committee also observed the names of distinguished individuals attached to the petition, who can scarcely be supposed to concur in its prayer : among which occurs the name of her Majesty, as Victoria Rex, April 1st [a laugh] ; F. M. Duke of Wellington, Sir Robert Peel, &c., &c. Your committee have also observed, in derogation of the value of such petition, the insertion of numbers of names which are obviously fictitious, such as " No Cheese," " Pug Nose," " Fat Nose " [roars of laughter]. There are others included, which your committee do not hazard offending the house and the dignity and decency of their own proceedings by reporting. It may be added that there are other signatures appended obviously belonging to the name of no human being " [cheers].

Schemes for Land and Liberty

Chartists formed a Land Company to help workers obtain and live off their own plots in small communes. It soon ran into debt and was dissolved.

Cheltenham Chronicle, January.

Yesterday morning some stir was created in the town by the arrival of a procession . . . connected with O'Connor and "the People's Land Scheme". The train consisted of a number of waggons filled with household furniture, wheat, potatoes, agricultural implements, and families of settlers on their way to the Chartist Estate at "Snig's End". There were about 30 horses in the teams—sleek, well-conditioned animals, but destined, we fear, to present a very different appearance after undergoing a few months connexion with the system of Chartist farming.

Chartist riot at Newport.

Anti-Chartist Propaganda

A typical passage from a newspaper put out by the government to spread the official viewpoint.

Voice of the People, 6 May.

We say, the demands of the Chartists are not genuine. Their whole conduct is a proof of our assertion. Their demand is for the possession of the franchise. *Have they, as individuals, ever endeavoured to acquire it?* The facts are these. The great proportion of the Chartists live, or are said to live, in the manufacturing towns of Lancashire and Yorkshire. In all these towns the occupation of a ten pound house, where the occupier pays the rates, confers the franchise. The houses inhabited by the factory population, and those engaged in the various subsidiary trades, and by mechanics—out of which classes nine-tenths of the so-called Chartists are drawn, or are said to be drawn—vary from £6 10s. to £9 of yearly rent; and of late many of a superior construction have been built, reaching ten pounds a year. Now, we have never seen nor heard of the manifestation of any wish, by these operatives, to become enfranchised, by dwelling in these higher-rented houses. It is true, these houses are eagerly sought, owing to their superior qualities, but the owners almost invariably pay the rates ; and we do not believe that ten instances have occurred in which the occupier has expressed a wish to pay the rates himself, for the sake of obtaining a vote. On the contrary, we have seen many instances of culpable indifference on their part to the possession of the franchise ; and we cannot easily forget how many refused even to pay the shilling which was demanded for the insertion of their name upon the registration list. It is not too much to say, that there are scarcely any, if any, operatives among the Chartists, who do not annually pay far more, in the form of subscriptions, to Chartist expenses, and Chartist delegates,—to say nothing of more sensual follies,—than would suffice to place them at once in possession of a ten pound house and a legal franchise. Chartism, we say boldly, is not the genuine expression, on the part of the respectable operatives, of a wish for the possession of the franchise for themselves ; it is a demand for universal suffrage on the part of those who hope to make their account out of the changes and confusion which must ensue.

A French View

Guizot was the reactionary French premier deposed in the January rising.

Letter from Guizot to Vitet, 1 July.

Everyone is delighted at this juncture there is a Whig ministry and a Conservative opposition. They argue that if the Whigs were in opposition they would be radicals, even Chartists, and there would be a new Reform Bill if not worse. The country is Conservative but timid, anxious as to the issue of a great struggle should it take place, looking back to the days of the mighty conflicts between Pitt and Fox as heroic times, long past, which it has no particular desire to see return, and hoping that a halt may be made at a cheaper rate on the slippery slope on which it feels itself placed. Maybe they are right.

" Lying, Filthy Press "

Throughout the summer, Chartists continued to gather for purposes lawful or unlawful. O'Connor continually urged peaceful methods.

Manchester Guardian, 14 June.

On Sunday last, a meeting of chartists was held on Blackstone Edge, convened for the purpose of replying to the statements of Lord John Russell and Mr. Cobden in the house of commons, to the effect that the people of this country were not desirous of any extensive reform. The proceedings commenced about two o'clock, when there were about ten thousand persons of the lowest classes present.

Mr. Shackleton proposed the first resolution, which was nearly as follows :—

" That this meeting, having heard the statements made by Lord John Russell in the house of commons, that the people of this country do not want the charter, that we throw back the foul libel, and further declare our firm conviction that no measure of reform is essential to good government, except that set forth in the above document, and that we never will relax our agitation until the charter becomes the law of the land."

Lord John Russell, in making the above observations, showed himself to be a black-hearted villain ; but he had probably been deceived by certain classes called newspaper writers—the lying, filthy press, which had misrepresented the opinions of the chartists on every occasion. If a civil revolution should take place, it would lie at the door of the press, as the conductors were the men who stood at the head of this mischief. Having abused, in no measured terms, the wealthy and middle classes of society, George James Clark, of Manchester, seconded the resolution. He was of opinion that the aristocracy of this country were going mad, and that the evil spirit mentioned in scripture, which was allowed to go forth in the mouths of the prophets to destroy Ahab, was doing the same now in the mouths of Lord John Russell and Mr. Cobden.

Policeman Murdered

Manchester Examiner, 15 August.

Last evening, about twelve o'clock, the town of Ashton was thrown into consternation and alarm by a report that the Chartists were intending to rise in insurrection at that hour, and from what occurred it would appear that the report was not without foundation. At about ten minutes before twelve, police constable James Bright was passing down Bentinck Street, and when about 50 yards below the Chartist room he was shot in the breast by some person at present not known to the authorities, although he must be known to at least 50 persons who were in company with the assassin, most of whom were armed with pikes or guns, and all were more or less armed with warlike arms of some kind or other. After this act of cold-blooded murder, the Chartist party pursued two other constables, who succeeded in evading them, and made their way to the Town Hall, from which a messenger was dispatched to the barracks, but on his proceeding about a quarter of a mile on the road he found it occupied by a number of men armed with pikes, who made him turn back. Another messenger was then dispatched who succeeded in gaining the barracks by a different route, when the military were immediately got under arms and brought out down towards where the mob had assembled. In the meantime the special constables had been called out, and with the borough police and several mounted special constables had attacked the armed mob, whom they put to flight, taking two of them prisoners. They also found a pyke on the road, the shaft of which is about 8 feet long, the blade about 12 inches long.

With a view to prevent any further outrages the soldiers were stationed in the Town Hall, while the special constables commenced a diligent search for arms. In their search they found a man who gave the name of William Healey of Newton Moor, a weaver, who had in his possession one pistol loaded, a butcher's steel, powder slugs, Chartist Manual, shot bag, pike head, wadding purse, a slater's pick sharpened, knife, and ramrod. A man named William Penny, who was in his company had some gun-caps in his possession ; a third named Thomas Lees, cotton-spinner, and who lives at Godley, had two boxes of lucifer matches ; a man named William Eden, a shoemaker, of Dunkinfield was also seized. He had in his possession one pike handle, two knives and two ball tickets. There were also several pikes and pike handles and other articles evidently made for the purpose of destroying life and of the most formidable description. There were altogether 22 persons apprehended for various offences.

The police were often brought out in force during the summer, to forestall riots.

Illustrated London News

Conspiracy?

Northern Star, 26 August and 7 October

Our town edition of last Saturday contained a report of the examination of the persons arrested in London on the preceding Wednesday. Two or three of the persons arrested, or said to be implicated, are known to have professed Chartist principles, and on this foundation the Press gang have been howling for a week past, over what they have called the " Discovery of a Chartist Conspiracy."

" Conspiracy " there may have been, but not a Chartist conspiracy. The only known Chartist against whom that charge is brought is Cuffay.

Now, taking the evidence against Cuffay for granted—which, in fact, considering the suspicious source it comes from, we are not inclined to do—it is rather too bad that one man's folly should be made the pretext for invoking vengeance against the entire Chartist party.

The truculent " *Times* "—true to its horrible reputation—has seized upon the recent trials at the Old Bailey as a pretext for renewed abuse and misrepresentation of Chartism, upon which it would fasten the odium of Powell's villany, and the folly of that miscreant's victims. In the first place it represents the " dozen or two tailors, shoemakers and joiners," tried at the Old Bailey, as the " nucleus and mainstay " of Chartism. In a subsequent article the " *Times* " says :— " The Chartists reckoned on the assistance of 50,000 thieves and rogues. They were assisted by one scoundrel more than they bargained for."

Right well the " *Times* " writers know that they lie when they represent the Chartists ₒas leagued with " thieves," or calculating upon the support of " rogues." We will not here, like some craven wretches, decry what is called " physical force." We always have asserted, and always will assert the right of the people everywhere and in all times to defend themselves from oppression and violence even by arms.

But we have ever deprecated the employment of physical force when other means of obtaining justice have been open to the oppressed ; and we have as ardently deprecated the very idea of any *section* of the people appealing to force, under any circumstances. We have done so, not because we are insensible to the rights of minorities, but because we are convinced that even a just cause and pure intentions are not sufficient to justify armed revolt. For any cause to be successful it must have the sanction of public opinion.

Two Years for a Speech

Illustrated London News, 2 September.

On Monday, *J. J. Bezer*, 38, was indicted for sedition. The Attorney-General, Mr. Welsby, Mr. Bodkin, and Mr. Clerk appeared for the Crown. The defendant had no counsel. The Attorney-General stated that the meeting at which the seditious speech was delivered was held on the 28th July, at the Milton-street Theatre, and at which more than a thousand persons were present ; and he reminded the jury that on the previous day there had been an unfounded report of a general rising of the people having taken place in Ireland, that the troops were disaffected and had been defeated. The meeting was convened by a placard, headed " Is Ireland up ?" and which went on to say that a great public meeting would be held that night, to take into consideration the present momentous crisis in Ireland. The Attorney-General proceeded to state that the defendant, who seemed to be a very clever person, and to possess very considerable ability, addressed the meeting, and read extracts from a most imflammatory character from one of the New York papers, thinking that by so doing he would evade the law. He was, however, very much mistaken in that respect. The Attorney-General then read the speech made by the defendant. The prisoner defended himself in an able speech ; after which Baron Platt summed up, and the jury immediately returned a verdict of " Guilty."

The other defendants, Snell, Crowe, and Bryson, who had been convicted of a similar offence, were thereupon ordered to be placed at the bar with the defendant who had been just convicted, to receive sentence. Baron Platt then sentenced George Snell, Robert Crowe, and John James Bezer to be imprisoned in the House of Correction for two years, to pay a fine of £10 each to the Queen, and at the expiration of their imprisonment to enter into their own recognisance in £100, to keep the peace for five years. The fourth defendant, Bryson, was sentenced to the same term of imprisonment, and to find the same amount of sureties for five years, and, in addition, to pay a fine of £20. When the sentence was pronounced, Bryson exclaimed to his companions, " Never mind, brother Chartists—come along." This attempt to cheer his comrades' spirits appeared to have very little effect.

Lord John Russell, the Whig prime minister, had supported the great Reform Bill and Catholic emancipation, but opposed the Chartists' demands for still further reforms.

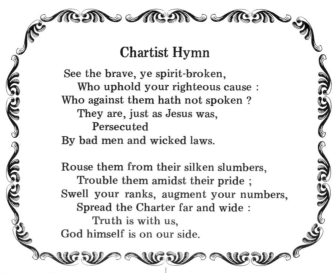

Chartist Hymn

See the brave, ye spirit-broken,
  Who uphold your righteous cause :
Who against them hath not spoken ?
  They are, just as Jesus was,
    Persecuted
By bad men and wicked laws.

Rouse them from their silken slumbers,
  Trouble them amidst their pride ;
Swell your ranks, augment your numbers,
  Spread the Charter far and wide :
    Truth is with us,
God himself is on our side.

Why Men Turned Chartist

Mrs. Gaskell's first novel, Mary Barton, illuminated even more than Disraeli's "Sybil" or Dickens' books, the reality of life in her neighbouring city, Manchester.

Fraser's Magazine (book review).

People on Turkey carpets, with their three meat meals a day, are wondering, forsooth, why working men turn Chartists and Communists.

Do they want to know why ? Then let them read Mary Barton. Do they want to know why poor men, kind and sympathising as women to each other, learn to hate law and order, Queen, Lords and Commons, country-party, and corn-law leagues, all alike—to hate the rich in short ? Then let them read Mary Barton Do they want to know what can madden brave, honest, industrious North-Country hearts, into self-imposed suicidal strikes, into conspiracy, vitriol-throwing, and midnight murder ? Then let them read Mary Barton.

Extract from Mary Barton

As they passed, women from their doors tossed household slops of *every* description into the gutter ; they ran into the next pool, which overflowed and stagnated. They picked their way till they got to some steps leading down into a small area, where a person standing would have his head about one foot below the level of the street, and might at the same time, without the least motion of his body, touch the window of the cellar and the damp muddy wall right opposite. You went down one step even from the foul area into the cellar in which a family of human beings lived. It was very dark inside. The window-panes were many of them broken and stuffed with rags, which was reason enough for the dusky light that pervaded the place even at mid-day. After the account I have given of the state of the street, no one can be surprised that on going into the cellar inhabited by Davenport, the smell was so foetid as almost to knock the two men down. Quickly recovering themselves, as those inured to such things do, they began to penetrate the thick darkness of the place, and to see three or four little children rolling on the damp, nay wet, brick floor, through which the stagnant, filthy moisture of the street oozed up ; the fire-place was empty and black ; the wife sat on her husband's chair, and cried in the dank loneliness.

THE
COMMUNIST
MANIFESTO

From the teachings of Marx sprang the secret Communist League (German), for which Marx and Engels wrote the Communist Manifesto. It helped to trigger off the French insurrection of June 1848, but was not published in England until 1850.

Mansell

Marx, left, a young journalist soon to be expelled from Prussia, collaborated in writing the Communist Manifesto with Engels, a wealthy German-born industrialist living in Manchester. The collaboration continued for life, with Engels often supporting Marx financially.

Engels Names It

Letter to Marx, 24 November 1847.

About the confession of faith. I believe it would be better if we dropped the form of a chatechism and entitled the thing : Communist Manifesto. In it, history must be told to a great or lesser degree and that does not suit its present form. I am bringing with me what I have done here—it is simple narrative but badly edited in a great hurry. I begin : What is Communism ? and then straight on to the Proletariat—history of origin, distinction from former workers, development of the opposition between the Proletariat and the Bourgeoisie, Crises, and deductions. In between this all kinds of secondary matters ; and finally, the policy of the Communist party as far as is necessary for the public. What I have here has not yet all been sanctioned, but I think, with the exception of a few small details, it will get through, so that at least there will be nothing in against our opinions.

Marx on the Mat

Resolution of the Communist League, 24 January.

The Central Committee hereby instructs the District Committee of Brussels to inform K. Marx that if the Manifesto of the Communist Party, which he agreed to draw up at the last congress [*Nov. 1847*], does not reach London by Tuesday, February 1st, further disciplinary measures will be taken against him. If K. Marx does not draw up the Manifesto, the Central Committee requests the immediate return of the documents which were handed over to him at the congress.

The Manifesto Published

It appeared in February : the first statement of a wholly working-class party, which regarded socialism as a middle-class movement. It began : " The history of all hitherto existing society is the history of class struggles " and closed with the now internationally famous cry " Workers of the world unite ". Here are extracts from the official English translation.

The bourgeoisie, wherever it has got the upper hand, has put an end to all feudal, patriarchal, idyllic relations. It has pitilessly torn asunder the motley feudal ties that bound man to his " natural superiors ", and has left remaining no other nexus between man and man than naked self-interest, than callous " cash payment ". It has drowned the most heavenly ecstasies of religious fervour, of chivalrous enthusiasm, of philistine sentimentalism, in the icy water of egotistical calculation.

The bourgeoisie, during its rule of scarce one hundred years, has created more massive and more colossal productive forces than have all preceding generations together. Subjection of Nature's forces to man, machinery, application of chemistry to industry and agriculture, steam-navigation, railways, electric telegraphs, clearing of whole continents for cultivation, canalisation of rivers, whole populations conjured out of the ground—what earlier century had even a presentiment that such productive forces slumbered in the lap of social labour ?

Owing to the extensive use of machinery and to division of labour, the work of the proletarians has lost all individual character, and, consequently, all charm for the workman. He becomes an appendage of the machine, and it is only the most simple, most monotonous, and most easily acquired knack, that is required of him.

The immediate aim of the Communists is the same as that of all the other proletarian parties : formation of the proletariat into a class, overthrow of the bourgeois supremacy, conquest of political power by the proletariat.

The distinguishing feature of Communism is not the abolition of property generally, but the abolition of bourgeois property.

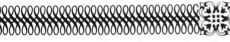

In the most advanced countries, the following will be pretty generally applicable :

1. Abolition of property in land and application of all rents of land to public purposes.

2. A heavy progressive or graduated income tax.

3. Abolition of all right of inheritance.

4. Confiscation of the property of all emigrants and rebels.

5. Centralisation of credit in the hands of the State, by means of a national bank with State capital and an exclusive monopoly.

6. Centralisation of the means of communication and transport in the hands of the State.

7. Extension of factories and instruments of production owned by the State ; the bringing into cultivation of waste-lands, and the improvement of the soil generally in accordance with a common plan.

8. Equal liability of all to labour. Establishment of industrial armies, especially for agriculture.

9. Combination of agriculture with manufacturing industries ; gradual abolition of the distinction between town and country, by a more equable distribution of the population over the country.

10. Free education for all children in public schools. Abolition of children's factory labour in its present form. Combination of education with industrial production, &c., &c.

The Communists disdain to conceal their views and aims. They openly declare that their ends can be attained only by the forcible overthrow of all existing social conditions. Let the ruling classes tremble at a Communistic revolution. The proletarians have nothing to lose but their chains. They have a world to win.

Right: In a cotton mill.

JOHN BULL'S ALIEN ACT.

Bull. " I 'LL ' PROPAGANDA' YOU, YOU MEDDLING FRENCH SCOUNDREL.   TAKE THAT—

Punch

The Aliens Act, passed in May, authorized the expulsion of foreign revolutionaries. To fears of a French invasion (fanned by Wellington's speeches) were added anxiety that Chartists and the Irish were in sympathy with the French revolutionaries, anger at the recent ejection from France of British workers, and mistrust of international Communist organisations, one of which (the Fraternal Democrats) had in February held a congress in London.

All Men are Brethren

The Fraternal Democrats (Communists), excited by the uprising in Paris, sent an address of support, rich in rhetorical flourishes.

Northern Star, 5 February.

Men of France

The signs of the times proclaim coming changes of vast magnitude and importance to your order.

We have watched with profound emotion those manifestations of progress and harbingers of popular triumph—the Reform Banquets—which have recently engaged the energies and talents of some of your most patriotic citizens. The " system " which at present presses like a vampire on the heart of France will in vain attempt by calumny and force to stay the progress of these manifestations. Any such attempts will but accelerate that crisis, in which the omnipotence of the popular sovereignty will prove the nothingness of renegades and traitors. It requires not the power of prophecy to foretell your speedy liberation from the degrading and disastrous yoke under which France has groaned for the last seventeen years.

In this country (Great Britain) the working millions, completely divided from the classes above them, are steadily

Mansell

The grim working conditions which existed in newly industrial cities were what had provoked the start of the Communist movement. (In a needle factory.)

advancing in political intelligence and political power ; and while perseveringly labouring for their own emancipation, they are not indifferent spectators of the grand struggle of which continental Europe is the theatre.

The patient and untiring labour of this people, with all the wonderful inventions and improvements in machinery and chemistry, which have produced for the master-classes their enormous masses of wealth, have brought for the working men only desolate homes, rags, hunger, and all the horrors of pauperism. As the manufacturers and merchants, and their allies, the usurers, have amassed wealth, in the same proportion that millions have become more and more impoverished, until the spectacle is presented of this richest of nations containing millions of its most industrious classes totally destitute of those social possessions which give men an interest in the institutions of the country they inhabit.

Is it to be wondered at that a wide gulf exists between those who possess all, and those who possess nothing ?

There have been congresses of Kings, let this year witness a congress of Peoples. At that congress let the union of nations be solemnized ; and let the ridiculous antipathies and barbarous enmities of the past be buried in oblivion. Frenchmen, Englishmen, Germans, Scandinavians, Poles, Russians, Italians, and men of all other lands, we appeal to you to embrace as brethren and march forward shoulder to shoulder, in the pursuit of *Equality*, *Liberty*, and *Fraternity*.

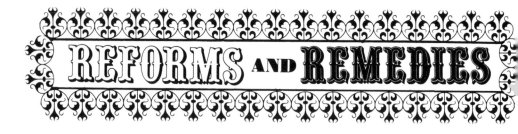

REFORMS AND REMEDIES

Although the Chartists were defeated and Communists driven underground, the nation recognized that reforms were urgently needed in the country's finances, its voting procedures and the conduct of its Parliament. Cobden (who earlier had led the successful fight against the protective Corn Laws) was campaigning for reductions in government expenditure ; while up and down the country middle-class progressives formed action groups to get the ballot extended and elections held more often than every 7 years (reforms which were not to be achieved until 1867 and 1911 respectively). But there was much bickering between the various Reform protagonists.

Class Co-operation

Typical of the many reforming societies now being set up was the Metropolitan Political Club—otherwise known as the Friends of Liberty, Order and Peace.

Club rules, 20 April.

Resident Suffrage

1.—To convene public meetings in London or in the country—to disseminate tracts, and institute lectures for the purpose of impressing on the Crown, the Government and the Legislature, the imperative necessity for an immediate extension of the elective franchise to all male residents who have attained the age of twenty-one years, who shall have been resident for the period of six months in the tenements for which they claim to vote. Provided that such persons are not in receipt of parochial relief, and are unconvicted of crime.

Qualification for Representatives

2.—That all born subjects of these realms shall be eligible to represent the people in parliament, provided their incomes are rated in such manner as the law directs, and at not less than the annual value of £200 and upwards, derived from trade, real estate, commercial or professional pursuits, and who shall obtain the majority of votes in the manner hereinafter indicated.

Mode of Voting—The Ballot

3.—That in order to protect the industrious and other classes from intimidation and loss, and to enable them to execute the elective franchise for the benefit of the community, their votes shall be taken by ballot.

Electoral Districts

4.—Perceiving the gross inequalities in numbers in the various constituencies of Great Britain and Ireland, this club deem it just that the country shall be divided into districts, and that population should be the basis on which the people ought to elect their representatives to parliament, therefore the club demand Equal Electoral Districts.

Duration of Parliaments

5.—Great injustice is perpetrated against the nation, in consequence of the law which empowers representatives to hold their seats for seven years. The average duration of septennial parliaments is scarcely three years, consequently, therefore, we consider that it would reconcile the working masses with the middle classes, by insisting on the abolition of the septennial act, and the enactment of a law, making the duration of parliament Triennial.

The Metropolitan Political Club earnestly request the co-operation of the middle classes with the working-men, in order to effect :

1st.—Resident Suffrage.
2nd.—Income Qualification for Members.
3rd.—Vote by Ballot
4th.—Equal Electoral Districts.
5th.—Triennial Parliaments.

Trafalgar Square was the scene of a mass demonstration against income-tax. The police tried to break it up (gatherings within a mile of Parliament were illegal) but were "assailed by missiles and groans". The demonstrators marched on Buckingham Palace, breaking lamp-posts as they went, but on seeing the guards turned out they dispersed.

Fewer Taxes

Cobden urged drastic cuts in escalating defence spending, so that some of the numerous duties and taxes on various goods might be reduced. It would take a long time, he thought, before income tax would be a popular alternative to these. 1848 was a year of four budgets and of countless protest meetings and demonstrations against taxes.

Letter from Cobden to Liverpool Reform Association, December.

The whole cost of the Government in [1835] was £44,422,000. For the twelve months ending the 5th April last, it amounted to £55,175,000, being an increase of £10,753,000. The estimated expenditure for the current year ending the 5th April, 1849 is £54,596,000 ; so that we may take the increase to be, in round numbers, £10,000,000 since 1835.—Do you see any good reason why we should not return to the expenditure of that

Lady's Newspaper

year ? Englishmen love precedents ; and they are not easily persuaded that anything is Utopian or impracticable which has been accomplished within the last thirteen years. In 1830, the last year of the Wellington-Peel administration, the expenditure for all purposes was £18,024,000 ; for the twelve months ending the 5th April of the present year, it amounted to £26,717,000. The Tory Government was overturned the following year in favour of economy, and the House of Commons was soon afterwards reformed, mainly on the plea of its profligate waste of the people's money ; and yet now we have an increase to the expenditure of £8,723,000, or nearly 50 per cent, as the fruits of the Reform Act. We are now actually expending more upon the army, navy, and ordnance alone, than sufficient for the maintenance of the whole civil and military establishments under the Duke of Wellington's government !

During the whole of last year, a fleet, as formidable as that required by the Americans to watch over their commerce in all parts of the globe, was maintained in the Tagus, out of the taxes of the British people, for the service of the Court and Government of Portugal. At this moment we have as large a fleet in the straits of Messina, engaged in an armed interference between the King of Naples and his Sicilian subjects, with no more interest or right on our part than the Government of the United States would have to send a squadron off Holyhead, and assume the character of an armed mediator between England and Ireland. For three or four years we have had a fleet in the River Plate, interfering in the endless and inexplicable squabbles of the Monte Videans and the Buenos Ayreans, and which has at last ended in a ridiculous failure. I would wish to see our Government spare the people this useless expense, by simply following the rule, observed by individuals, of leaving other nations to settle their quarrels, and minding its own business better.

It would be far easier to effect a reduction of expenditure to the extent of £10,000,000, and apply the whole of that sum to the removal of Excise and Customs duties, than to transfer the same amount from indirect to direct taxation. Excepting in Liverpool and a few of our largest trading towns, there is not, at present, a very great force of public opinion in favour of direct taxation. It has yet to be created and organized.

Proposed reductions:

	Loss of
CUSTOMS DUTIES.	Revenue.
Tea—Duty to be reduced to one shilling per pound	£2,000,000
Timber and Wood— Duty abolished	945,000
Butter, cheese, and upwards of one hundred smaller items of the tariff —Duties abolished	516,000

Total loss upon Customs £3,461,000

EXCISE DUTIES.

Malt—Duty abolished	...	£4,260,000	
Hops— ,,	,,	...	416,000
Soap— ,,	,,	...	850,000
Paper— ,,	,,	...	720,000

Total loss on Excise ;.......... £6,246,000

TAXES.

Window Tax— Abolished	£1,610,000
Advertisement Duty— Abolished	160,000

Total of Taxes £1,770,000

Reductions a Dream

Illustrated London News, 5 February.

The invasion fever seems to have had the effect of reconciling the public to a greater outlay of money on military preparations, as a necessity ; but we apprehend our expenditure under this head will not be very largely increased at once. An addition to the Artillery, and a calling out of the Militia to the number of ten thousand men each year, are said to be the extent of the martial preparations we are to make. We may bid a long farewell to all hopes of that dream of the heavily burdened—a reduction of taxation. The Tea Duties are vainly represented to the polite, but somewhat frigid Premier, as unequal, oppressive, and everything that a tax always is when people wish to get rid of it. " The answer is as ready as the borrower's cap :" we can't spare the money. To the abolishers of the Window Tax the same

JOHN BULL BETWEEN PEACE AND WAR.

Peace - - - Mr. Cobden.   *War* - - - The Dook.

Punch

John Bull is torn between the French invasion warnings of Wellington, and the disarmament policy advocated by Cobden.

reply is given ; and there is a decisive, cold unanswerability about the plea of poverty, which disarms opposition. As less taxation is impossible, and as more money is wanted, it remains to enquire what new impost is to be laid on, or what old one is to be increased. Two and two is not always four in finance ; for doubling the per centage of a tax does not produce twice the former revenue from it. These are the problems with which the Chancellor of the Exchequer has to meet the Parliament of 1848.

Liberal MP, and leader of Corn Law repeal in earlier years, Cobden now campaigned for fewer taxes and less government interference. He opposed privilege (whether of class or of trade union) ; supported disarmament.

RTHPL

29

Mr. Bull. "HOLLO! YOU SIR! WHERE ARE YOU GOING WITH THAT INCREASED INCOME-TAX?"   John Russell. "BOCK AGIN."

Punch

Protest Meeting

Weekly Times, 5 March.

Immense assemblage took place in Freemasons'-hall to protest against the Government proposition to increase the income tax. The following petition will be read with profit :— " That the petitioners have observed with feelings of the most painful nature that her Majesty's Ministers have proposed to burden the industry of the nation by increasing the income tax. They perceive with extreme mortification that her Majesty's Ministers, in opposition to the wishes of the people, persist in the continuance of that unjust and arbitrary system of class-legislation which extracts the revenue of the country from the industrial, instead of the wealthier classes. The recent financial crisis, and stagnation in commerce, and consequent increase of crime, mortality, destitution, and disease throughout the country, are clearly to be traced to an unjust and oppressive system of class-legislation, which your petitioners were led to expect her Majesty's Ministers would have abolished immediately after their accession to office. That the prosperity of an empire and the happiness of a people can only be attained by removing the taxes from all the necessaries of life,—such as bread, tea, sugar, coffee, malt, soap, &c. The petitioners earnestly hope that her Majesty's Ministers will see the necessity of abandoning their intended project of adding to the income-tax. This petition, it is unnecessary to repeat, was carried unanimously. It was afterwards signed by 1,240 persons.

Taxes on Health

Illustrated London News, 20 May.

Independently of the question of a further reform in Parliament, upon which opinion is much divided, there is one great question upon which opinion is unanimous, and upon which a very considerable agitation has already arisen throughout the country : reform of our fiscal system, and the diminution of our national expenditure. Taxation has reached its limit. Collection of the national revenue draws from the pockets of the people large sums, which are stopped *in transitu*, and never find their way to the national Exchequer. Every ten millions of taxation costs, directly or indirectly, one million and a half to collect. In addition to this evil, we impose taxes upon articles which ought not to be taxed ; we levy a rate upon light and air by our window duties ; we place an impost upon cleanliness by the Excise duty upon soap ; and we increase the price of articles of prime necessity by injudicious taxes. We also tax trade by our Stamp Acts, and by our stamp on newspapers and the advertisement duty. Moreover, while we tax the succession to personal property at a heavy rate, the succession to real property pays nothing to the necessities of the State. Associations formed with the sole object of urging financial reform upon the attention of the legislature are arising in all the great manufacturing and commercial districts.

Britain for the Birds

Jews were prevented from becoming MP's by having to swear a Christian oath first. But the Bill to remove this disability failed to get passed in 1848.

Weekly Times, 30 January.

A numerously attended public meeting was held, at the Horns Tavern, Kennington, to take measures in favour of Lord John Russell's bill for the removal of Jewish disabilities. Mr. Dixon moved :— " That this meeting observes with satisfaction that a bill has been introduced into the House of Commons, by Lord John Russell, having for its object the removal of many of the disabilities now imposed on the Jews." The Rev. J. Burnett seconded the resolution. He thought it absurd to say that because the Jews were descended from Abraham they were not to have a seat in the Legislature. He asked what we were all descended from ? Who were the real aborigines—who were indigenous to the soil ? He suspected that we were all importations, and if the English people were to go to its own races for laws and government, some would be obliged to go to the Huns, some to the Normans—some

to the one end of the world, and some to the other—and Britain would be left, as before, to the birds. Mr. Thornborough moved the last resolution, which was, adopting a petition in accordance with the views which had been expressed, and appointing a committee.

Liberty of the Individual

Civil servant and philosopher J. S. Mill's first book reflected his father's Utilitarianism : an intellectual and extreme statement of individual freedom. Later, he drew nearer to liberal socialism.

Extract from Principles of Political Economy.

There is a spontaneous education going on in the minds of the multitude, which may be greatly accelerated and improved by artificial aids. The instruction obtained from newspapers and political tracts is not the best sort of instruction, but it is vastly superior to none at all. The institutions for lectures and discussion, the collective deliberations on questions of common interest, the trades unions, the political agitation, all serve to awaken public spirit, to diffuse variety of ideas among the mass, and to excite real thought and reflection in a few of the more intelligent, who become the leaders and instructors of the rest. Although the too early attainment of political franchises by the least educated class might retard, instead of promoting, their improvement, there can be little doubt that it is greatly stimulated by the attempt to acquire those franchises. It is of little importance that some of them may, at a certain stage of their progress, adopt mistaken opinions. Communists are already numerous, and are likely to increase in number ; but nothing tends more to the mental development of the working classes than that all the questions which Communism raises should be largely and freely discussed by them ; nothing could be more instructive than that some should actually form communities, and try practically what it is to live without the institution of property. In the meantime, the working classes are now part of the public ; in all discussions on matters of general interest they, or a portion of them, are now partakers ; all who use the press as an instrument may, if it so chances, have them for an audience ; the avenues of instruction through which the middle classes acquire most of the ideas which they have, are accessible to, at least, the operatives in the towns. With these resources, it cannot be doubted that they will increase in intelligence, even by their own unaided efforts ; while there is every reason to hope that great improvements both in the quality and quantity of school education, will be speedily effected by the exertions of government and of individuals, and that the progress of the mass of the people in mental cultivation, and in the virtues which are dependent on it, will take place more rapidly, and with fewer intermittences and aberrations, than if left to itself.

A daguerreotype of J. S. Mill.

Mansell

A PUBLIC STINK

At the beginning of the century, only one person in ten lived in a town ; but soon the new factories, offering doubled earnings, attracted thousands of workers to each town. The result was appalling overcrowding in hastily built houses. The well and earth-closet adequate in village life were wildly insanitary in these conditions ; and there was no way to dispose of rubbish except by throwing it into the street (or a stream, the source of drinking-water). Soon cholera outbreaks focused public alarm on the problem, and Chadwick led a campaign for proper sewers to be provided. The result was the Public Health Act which recognized the government's responsibility for sewage disposal and a piped water-supply. Under it, a central board was empowered to set up local boards to supervise sanitation etc, either on the petition of local citizens or compulsorily if the death rate exceeded 2.3%. For London, a separate Sewers Bill was drafted.

Example to Europe

The Public Health Act was not far-reaching in itself, but was important because it was the first time that a government, galvanized into action by rising mortality figures and a cholera scare, recognized any responsibility in this field.

Times (Parliamentary report), 1 July.

Lord Campbell rose to move the second reading of the bill. The bill was one of great importance to all classes, but more particularly to the poor, and therefore it might not inappropriately be called the poor man's measure. To show the ill effects resulting from a crowded population, attended with its usual concomitants of filth and bad ventilation, he contrasted 10,000 of the population of agricultural Westmoreland with 10,000 of that of manufacturing Lancashire. In Westmoreland, 23 out of the 10,000 died of epidemic diseases. In Lancashire, the number who died from the same cause was

53. Of the Westmoreland population, the number of deaths in the 10,000 from diseases of the respiratory organs was 47 ; in the Lancashire population it was 73. The deaths of persons between the ages of 20 and 60 were, in Westmoreland, 49 ; in Lancashire, 68. The deaths in the whole 10,000 were, in Westmoreland, 206 ; in Lancashire, 279. The evidence collected by the Sanitary Commission showed that frightful disease and mortality prevailed in the manufacturing districts, owing to the non-adoption of precautions for the preservation of health. It was impossible, he said, to point to a more striking proof of the benefit resulting from good drainage, sewerage, ventilation, and a plentiful supply of water than was furnished by the present condition of the prisons of this country. Their lordships must have often heard of that terrible scourge, the gaol fever, which used to carry off not only prisoners, but persons whom business drew to the assizes, counsel, witnesses, and jurymen. Now, however, in consequence of the sanitary regulations adopted in the prisons, they were, generally, more healthy than any part of the country. A document which he held in his hand showed, that in a district in which the deaths were 1 in 32, the construction of sewers had, in a single year, reduced the mortality to 1 in 39. The model lodging-houses formed another proof of what could be done in the way of sanitary improvement. Yet little had been done to promote this great object—the public health ; and the poor had in consequence been subjected to very serious sufferings.

The present bill would constitute a general board of health, which would appoint inspectors to make the proper investigations with a view to carrying the bill into effect. On the petition of a certain proportion of the inhabitants of any place, this bill might be applied to that district. Then there would be local boards of health in the various districts ; these boards would consist of the town councillors, where a municipal borough constituted the district, and elsewhere of persons elected by the ratepayers. These boards would have the management of the sewerage, drainage, cleansing, and various other matters, and, above all, the supply of water. In this part of the bill there were some provisions with regard to interments, which he (Lord Campbell) was sorry to hear would be disapproved in their present shape by some of the right rev. prelates ; he could only say, that any suggestion from them for otherwise effecting the object in view would be most respectfully received and considered.

The Cost of Health

Now, what were the objections to the bill ? He had heard the expense mentioned as one ; but he believed that in many cases there would be a considerable sum realized by turning to account water and manure, which were now wasted, and at the same time the poor-rates would be lowered by the prevention of sickness and disease, saving expenditure for medical aid, for children, now left to be maintained in the workhouses, and for the support of persons reduced to premature old age. It was objected also that the bill did not include London. It excluded, not the city in particular, but the whole of the metropolitan district. When Parliament should legislate for the metropolis, he hoped they would legislate for the city. He should be very sorry if the city were to set up what were called its privileges and immunities to mar such a measure. But, in existing circumstances, it was prudent to postpone the bill for the metropolis. There were such peculiarities in its case, that it could not have been included in the same bill with the rest of England. There were eight or ten different commissions of sewers, and a number of drainage boards, and the machinery applicable generally would not be adapted to London. A bill for the metropolis was in preparation, the result of very diligent inquiry ; the bill was being prepared under the superintendence of Mr. Chadwick, to whom great praise was due for his unwearied industry in this cause (hear, hear).

He trusted, however, that the present bill, so far as it went would need the approbation of their lordships and that they would set an example to Europe of an anxiety to improve the condition of the lower orders, not holding out to them vain promises and expectations, but offering what would be really performed. For the first time a legislature was framing a law for the general health of the community.

Illustrated London News

Edwin Chadwick, though a repressive Poor Law administrator, campaigned effectively for sanitary reform.

Governments would be much better employed in trying to improve the social condition of the people than in revolutionary measures, or in trying to bring about what was really beyond their power to accomplish. (Hear, hear.)

Apparatus for clearing cess-pools.

The Polluted Environment

Typical of the mounting public and private concern expressed in the papers was this letter from an unscientific nose.

Times (reader's letter) 28 July, and Builder, 24 June.

Sir,—On going to the Rolls' Court this morning I found the porter carefully stopping up all the street gratings near the place, and he informed me that the smell which came from them was utterly unbearable. Though I perused with great respect the extracts which appeared in your paper a few days ago containing minute calculations on the area of cesspools in London and the smell assumed to be attendant thereon, I could not help considering whether it was not possible that an unscientific nose might not prefer the cesspools which it was not able to smell to the drains which now attack it at each grating.

I am, Sir, a Barrister.

At the last census in 1841 there were 270,859 houses in the metropolis. It is known that there is scarcely a house without a cesspool under it ; and that very many old houses have two, three, and more. The exposed surface of each cesspool, taken on an average, measures 9 feet ; and the mean depth of the whole is about 6½ feet. The exhaling surface of all the cesspools equals 62 acres nearly. If such a gigantic cesspool of filth were to be seen, it would fill the mind with horror ; but, as is shown above, a vast number of

---

A vast survey of London was undertaken as a preliminary to laying out a new sewer system, with observation platforms mounted on church pinnacles and army engineers surveying the streets.

Engineer. "DON'T BE ALARMED, MA'AM, IT'S ONLY A DUMPY LEVELLER."
Old Lady. "LAW! DEAR NOW! WELL, I'M SURE I THOUGHT IT WAS A BLUNDERBUST. BUT DON'T FIRE IT OFF, YOUNG MAN, TILL I'M GOT BY, FOR I WAS ALWAYS TERRIBLE FEARED OF GUNS."

Punch

small ones, which, added together, equal it in extent, is dotted all over the town. From them a nasty, stinking, pestiferous vapour is constantly escaping, corrupting the atmosphere from one end of London to the other, and creating disease, misery, poverty.

Obnoxious Serpentine
Times, 9 August.

Although complaints have been made, and justly, of the very dirty and stinking state of the Serpentine river, at the west end of the waters in Kensington-gardens, yet nothing seems to be done, or attempted to be effected, in order to remedy this glaring evil. It really seems a pity that this handsome piece of water, should be left in such a shameful state, as not only to be most unpleasing to the eye, but actually, from its stagnant condition, rendered most obnoxious to the sense. The cause of such a state of things need not again be

sixteen houses had been inspected in which contagious diseases had existed—three for the second time. On six of the occupying tenants notices of the necessary reformations had been served ; six other similar notices had been sent to the landlords, and in three of the remaining four these sanitary improvements had been made by the committee. The district medical attendants' reports were next considered, reporting for the week in five of the sections twenty cases of fever, sixteen of diarrhoea, and one of English cholera. The present aspect of Asiatic cholera was then taken up. It appears from authentic reports that it is steadily and rapidly advancing westward, and thus progressing toward us, and that unless God, in His providence, prevent, we may look for its visit as certain, and perhaps as soon. Where it entered, its severity was excessive. At St. Petersburg, in *nine* days, ending 3d July, there had been 5,063 cases, or 562 cases daily, of which 2,596, or more than a-half had proved fatal—at Jassey, from the

A SNAKE IN THE SEWERS.

The Sanitary Commissioners' leather hoses became a commonplace sight in the streets.

Punch

mentioned, and we can hardly bring ourselves to believe that means might not be easily and speedily adopted to turn the course of the foul collection into its proper channel.

Cholera and Cleanliness
Banner of Ulster, 25 July.

The weekly meeting of the inspection committee of the Sanitary Society was held. The report of the society's inspector was considered. Many most useful improvements in the sewerage, were reported as progressing. During the week

17th to the 28th June, 1,799 persons had been attacked, and 810 of them, or a-half had died—in Bucharist, 23d June, the number of cases was 186 a-day, of whom a fifth are rapidly carried off. It is thus spreading with fearful rapidity and fatality over Poland and Hungary as well as Russia. It was finally resolved " that this committee hereby earnestly request ' the officers of health ' to issue a general and public notice on the importance and necessity for cleanliness specially amongst the poor—as peculiarly necessary at the present time, when seemingly threatened with cholera.

Dead Dogs and Dung

Times (quoting from a sewer inspector's report),
7 August.

We have inspected some of the sewers in the Surrey and Kent division. The district to which we confined our attention was densely populated, and by classes differing widely in their position in society.

The sewers in this district may be divided into two distinct classes, the low level and the high level lines ; those designated as the " low levels " are placed deep below the surface, and are the main lines. In all of this description that we have inspected the falls are very defective ; frequently they are the reverse way, forming hollows, in which there are constant accumulations of deposit. The general inclinations appear to be of small amount ; they are filled to a considerable distance, and for many hours at high tide with the " back-water," or natural drainage ; during these periods matters which the ordinary current holds in suspension are constantly deposited.

The " inverts " of those sewers designated as " high levels " are from four to five feet below the surface ; they appear to have been the natural water-courses or drainage-ditches. The two levels may be distinguished thus : " the high level " as natural surface drains, the " low level " as main sewers formed artificially for the drainage of the houses and for the reception of the " high levels." The " high levels " pass over the " low levels " in many places, ultimately falling into them by sudden perpendicular descents or drops of from six to seven feet. In many places these ditches, the " high levels," are open, running at the backs of the houses, the walls of which frequently form the sides of the ditch.

In many of the houses the bedroom windows open over the ditches, and are at a height from the foul deposit of not more than from seven to twelve feet ; from these windows offal and refuse of every kind is thrown into the ditch. In parts the top or crown of the ditch (or sewer) is formed by the flooring of rooms in which there are residents, as we found by hearing the people talk and by seeing them through the cracks of the boarding above our heads.

The greater part of the houses on the sides or over these sewers have privies opening direct into them, either through the sides or crown ; they are frequently in a dilapidated and most disgusting condition the ceilings of many are visible from the sewer.

Sodden Walls

The foundations of the walls of the houses forming their sides are in many parts sodden and in a ruinous condition ; large vacuities are formed by the falling in of the brickwork, the materials displaced being deposited in the sewer.

The sewers are receptacles of the refuse of the houses, as almost every kind which can be imagined is found in them in abundance ; they are, in fact, the only dust-bins of some localities. It will thus appear that the fluid drainage passing into them must of necessity stagnate, and aid in the decomposition of the more solid matter. The deposit comprises amongst other ingredients from manufactories, &c., dead dogs and cats, offal from slaughter-houses, vegetable refuse, stable dung, privy soil, ashes, tin kettles and pans, broken stone-ware, as jars, pitchers, &c., bricks, pieces of wood, &c. ; add to this that there is a constant discharge of hot water and steam from many manufactories, the effect of the decomposition in the emission of noxious gases must be baneful to an alarming extent.

The deposit varies in depth from two or three inches to as many feet, and is frequently under the foundations of the houses.

On a part of one line which is at the back of and parallel to the houses in a court there are small yards, formed by platforms of loose boarding laid over the ditch. We need hardly remark that the general appearance of those ditches was disgusting in the extreme, and that the smells in many parts were high nauseous.

So accustomed, it would appear, are the residents in the vicinity to the emanations from those places that those of whom we made inquiry stated that they did not perceive any smells, were not annoyed, and thought that their health was not affected by them ; we would, however, beg to observe that, in the majority of cases, their looks betokened a condition anything but confirmatory of these statements.

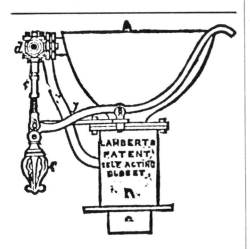

A rarity in 1848: "patent self-acting water-closet."
Health of Towns Journal, 11 November.

Foul and Black, Bubbling and Hissing

Times, 21 August.

The old proverb, "*omne ignotum pro mirifico,*" is not of universal application. There are some things which require not only to be seen, but also to be smelt before they can produce their full effect on the organ of wonder. Some of Her Majesty's lieges inhabiting the borough of Southwark have recently been thrown into a state of " alarm " by finding their noses woefully offended as they passed some new sewers' gratings in the streets ; and in order to make that alarm impressive on the world at large they have embodied it in a parochial resolution requesting the Commissioners of Sewers to hold their hands. If these alarmists had any knowledge of the actual state of the subterranean regions of the borough, their alarm would be natural enough, but it would exhibit itself in another direction. They are living over a mass of the foulest poison, which is incessantly contaminating with its deadly influences the air they breathe. Many years of the grossest neglect of their duty on the part of the former Commissioners of

Sewers have resulted in the accumulation in the sewers, drains, ditches, and cesspools of Southwark and its neighbourhood of hundreds of thousands of tons of night-soil and sullage. To let that accumulation remain is altogether out of the question. To allow the gases which are generated by its decomposition to continue to poison the air of the houses into which it directly ascends would be to connive at manslaughter. The filth must, somehow or other, be removed, and the escape of the gases into houses must, if possible, be prevented. To do either cannot but be a work of time. Mitigation of the evils must be attempted in the first instance. If these parochial alarmists would point out how the filth could be got rid of, and the disease and deaths which it is daily occasioning could be prevented, without annoyance to the olfactories of themselves or their neighbours, they would do good service to the State, and might then turn their hands, with a tolerably fair prospect of success, to the transmutation of metals. But until the Scotch proverb, " the more stir, the more stink," loses its credibility, the performance of the Augean task which has been thrown on the shoulders of the new Commissioners of Sewers cannot but occasion local inconvenience.

Strong Man Faints

A recent examination by one of the assistant-surveyors of the Commissioners into the condition of sewers in Blackfriars-road and Friar-street was reported on at the last Court. With two men he went into the Friar-street sewer, which was built by the late commissioners last year. In less than five minutes all the money in their purses, their watches, and other metal articles which they had with them, were completely discoloured. The silver money was exhibited at that Court. It was almost black. One of the men fainted, and fell into the sullage, which was upwards of 2 feet deep, and the others were so much affected by the gases that they had great difficulty in recovering him and escaping from the sewer.

" Every part of the exposed surface of the sewer was covered with a white efflorescence. The water in the sewer was covered with air bubbles ; it appeared in some places actually to boil : there was a continual hissing produced by the generation of these bubbles. The sewer was filled to an average depth of 2 feet 2 inches with very foul, black, stinking water."

This almost new sewer is nearly on a dead level ; in some places it has a fall the wrong way, and it has a barrier of 1 foot 10 inches in height at its junction with the outfall sewer. Unless it be altered, it must always retain sullage to the depth of about 2 feet throughout its whole length ; and unless some steps be taken to cleanse it, the bubbling and hissing of the poisonous gases generated in it, and their deleterious effects on the health of the inhabitants, must be perpetuated. What is to be done ? Are the new Commissioners to follow the *laissez faire* plan of their predecessors, and to build more sewers with the fall the wrong way and blocked up outfalls ? Surely, gentlemen of Southwark, this would not content you !

Filth Breeds Fever

Weekly Times, 5 March.

On Monday an inquest was held before Mr. Mills, at the Boots, Cromer-street, Brunswick-square, upon John Donnelly, an Irish labourer, late of Union-court, Compton-street, who died of typhus fever. The inquest was held in consequence of a report that deceased's death was the result of the fetid, unwholesome atmosphere in which he lived. From the general evidence it appeared that in a room six feet square deceased, his wife, and six children resided, who were all seized with typhus fever. There were within the same court where they lived 500 Irish of the lowest character, and fever constantly raged in the vicinity. Doctors Popham and Walters examined the court, which they found to be a sink of filth, full of stagnant cesspools, and totally deprived of ventilation and light ; in fact, a very hotbed of infection. They were of opinion that the fever of which deceased died, and which raged in the court, was the result of its filthy, crowded condition. The jury returned a verdict in accordance with the medical testimony, accompanied by an earnest desire that the owners of the premises would without delay abate the dangerous nuisance that prevailed in the court, and

render its houses fit habitations for human beings, adopting efficient measures to induce the tenants and their lodgers to maintain in their houses cleanliness and good order. The governors of the Foundling Hospital are the owners of this filthy congregation of dwellings unfit for human abode.

Crowd Diseases Spreading

Illustrated London News, 13 May.

The Registrar-General issued his quarterly statement on Wednesday last :— The population was 6,612,958 in 1841. The mortality has been high in the quarter ending March 31, 1848, and, taking the increase of population into account, higher than in the corresponding quarter of the year 1847. The deaths returned were 57,710. The smallest number of deaths returned in the ten last winter quarters was 42,410, in 1839. In 1847, scurvy, typhus, and other zymotic diseases prevailed ; and at the end of the year influenza broke out. Its ravages extended over the country, and continued in some districts through the month of January, 1848. Typhus is still epidemic in London, and destroys the lives of from 60 to 80 persons weekly. Small-pox, measles, scarlatina, and hooping-cough were fatal to many. The deaths ascribed to influenza in the thirteen weeks were 102, 102, 89, 56, 29, 47, 27, 33, 18, 11, 10, 16, 8. Pulmonary diseases (exclusive of consumption) were little more than half as fatal at the end as they were at the beginning of the quarter. A great difference will be observed in the causes of death in 1847 and 1848, although the mortality was high in both winters. In the winter of 1847 the deaths from diseases of the lungs were 4056 ; in 1848 they were 3357 ; on the other hand, zymotic diseases were more than twice as fatal in 1848 as they were in 1847.

The deaths in the districts of Lancashire and Cheshire, in the five winters, were nearly equal, in the last two years, to the deaths in London, although the population was only 1,530,460 in 1841, when the population of London was 1,948,369. From the registrar's remarks, it appears that typhus, scarlatina, hooping-cough, and smallpox were epidemic in many parts of the country. The mortality of Birmingham, Manchester, and Liverpool still remains excessively high. The deaths in Birmingham were 1660 ; the population was 138,187 in 1841. Birmingham has, in its site, many advantages in a sanatory point of view, and the occupations of the people are not insalubrious ; but the beneficence of nature appears to be defeated by the negligence of the authorities. Water, pure air, and a perfect system of drainage are not provided, as they might be, for the whole town ; and the consequence is that want and the epidemics abroad have destroyed thousands of the lives of the inhabitants within the last two years. The fatal effects of collecting large bodies of labourers, without adequate house accommodation, have been illustrated in Lincoln.

The increase of a temporary population connected with the formation of railways, without a sufficient increase of accommodation, has induced typhus and measles.

The extent to which vaccination is neglected in some parts of the country is deplorable and inconceivable. Such facts as the following are, it is to be feared, not uncommon in other districts besides East Sunderland :— " Deaths, 140 ; considerably above the average ; 69 more than in the corresponding quarter of last year. The

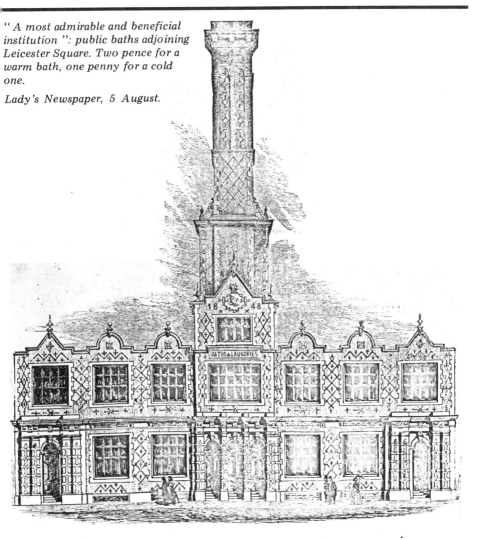

" A most admirable and beneficial institution ": public baths adjoining Leicester Square. Two pence for a warm bath, one penny for a cold one.

Lady's Newspaper, 5 August.

increase is principally to be attributed to the prevalence of small-pox in the district. 47 persons have died of small-pox, (only one after vaccination.) Out of the 140 deaths 84 are under five years."

Here 47 persons, chiefly children, died ; and this implies that some hundreds besides were injured and disfigured, by a disease that may be almost altogether prevented by vaccination ; which the legislature, under the administration of the Poor-law, has placed within the reach of every poor child in the kingdom.

Pigs and Dwellings
Illustrated London News, 6 September.

On Monday, cautions were extensively circulated in Bethnal-green and White-chapel, warning persons of the penalties incurred by keeping pigs near dwelling-houses. Such nuisances are very common in that locality. In the parish of St. Ann, Westminster, the inhabitants were publicly warned not to cast refuse or offal into the public street. At Leadenhall Market notice was issued that no raw or undressed hides would be allowed to be brought into, or remain in the market before or after the market days.

Only one Hospital for Lung Cases
Illustrated London News, 8 January.

An institution has just been founded, under the title of " The Central Metropolitan Dispensary," to provide for the poor who are afflicted by diseases of the stomach, heart, and lungs, including consumption, asthma, &c. London has but one hospital for the reception of consumptive patients, although their case is most distressing and disastrous, the public returns of mortality testifying to the fact that more deaths are caused by this fatal disease than by any other to which humanity is exposed.

Royal Support for Baths for the Poor
Illustrated London News and Health of Towns Journal, 11 November.

Baths and wash-houses for the labouring classes.—On Wednesday a meeting of the subscribers and supporters of the above institution, founded for the benefit of the labouring classes in the north-west districts of the metropolis, was held. The report congratulated the subscribers on the results, since its formation in 1846. During the last month the number of bathers had been 16,143 ; and 16,196 poor women have washed, dried, ironed and mangled the clothes of themselves and families— representing on an average near 300,000 cases annually deriving the benefit of the institution. The present building being totally inadequate for its purposes, hundreds are daily turned away for want of accommodation. The institution itself has been self-supporting since its establish-ment. The subscription towards its extension ranks amongst its members her Majesty and Prince Albert, the Archbishop of Canterbury, and a number of highly distinguished individuals.

The probable supply of the 1,000,000 inhabitants of which Rome could at one time boast, amounted to 50,000,000 cubic feet, being equal to about 50 cubic feet for each individual. This is probably 20 times the quantity which London now receives for each of its inhabitants—a fact which goes far to justify the application of the disgraceful term " bathless," to this the largest, the most opulent, and the most powerful city in the world.

Cholera Approaches

This was the second epidemic of the dreaded killer-disease, so little understood that it was attributed to miasma (unhealthy vapours), the weather, even the absence of thunderstorms to charge the air with electricity. Panic at its onset accelerated the cause of sanitary reform ; but some remedies applied to its victims only added to their suffering.

Illustrated London News, 26 February and 28 October.

The Sanatory Commissioners' Report was presented on Wednesday. The following are their latest results of inquiries :—

Having received much additional

information as to the progress of cholera towards Europe, and as to the means of its prevention, we find :—

That the disease, as it has recently appeared in Persia, Trebizonde, and in Russia, is in a similar position to that in which it was in 1831, when its progress was arrested by the frost, previously to its advance upon Europe immediately after the thaw took place.

That the more recent experience in Russia has led to the general abandonment of the theory of its propagation by contagion.

That the inexpediency of special Cholera Hospitals has been confirmed by the same conclusions in Russia.

That cholera is not the sudden disease which has hitherto been supposed ; that the commonly-known form of the malady is, in reality, its second stage ; and that its first stage is manifested by the premonitory symptom of diarrhoea, which is commonly unattended to.

That we recommend preparation be made for the establishment of local dispensaries, where persons affected with the first stage of the disease may be immediately placed under proper treatment.

Having examined, as closely as the time and means at our disposal would permit, the late extraordinary increase of mortality in the metropolis, amounting in eleven weeks to 6145 deaths above the usual average, an excess of mortality during those eleven weeks greater than the entire mortality from the cholera in the metropolis during the twenty-one weeks when it prevailed in the year 1832, we find—

That sickness and mortality from diarrhoea and from typhus of precisely the same type as that which preceded the former visitation of cholera, have been excessive amongst the population of the low, ill-drained, ill-cleansed, and over-crowded neighbourhoods that are marked as the cholera tracts of 1832.

That the inmates of a model lodging-house, and the prisoners in the chief prisons in the metropolis, where the drainage, cleansing, dryness, ventilation, and warmth, are better than ordinary, have been distinguished by proportionate immunity from typhus, influenza, and other epidemic diseases, affording an exemplification of the freedom from such disease, which would probably follow the extension of similar sanatory arrangements.

That in the lower, the ill-drained and the worst cleansed districts, in the close streets, courts, and alleys, chiefly occupied by the poorer population, typhus and other epidemics, are now prevalent, with an increasing frequency and intensity.

That, there being no systematic land drainage, and no proper pre-appointed system for the drainage of land intended to be used for the sites of houses, a great part of the drainage from the suburban houses is carried into open stagnant ditches.

That in one of these marshes the proportion of open ditch is 18½ to 350 acres, or 1 acre of ditch to 24 acres of land ; stagnating and giving off emanations from the decomposition of animal as well as vegetable refuse ; and that in the Surrey district of sewers alone there are nearly 70 miles of uncovered ditches and open watercourses, complained of as being stagnant, as receiving house drainage, and as giving off much offensive moisture.

Some isolated cases of cholera have been reported during the week. Relative to the convict ships off Woolwich. Mr. Rixon, the registrar of the sub-district, Woolwich Arsenal, makes the following statement :— " The seven deaths from Asiatic cholera registered by me last week occurred in the *Unité* hospital ship, among convicts from the *Justitia* hulk, lying off the Royal Arsenal wharf. The surgeon attributes the disease to the unhealthy state of the atmosphere and to the locality—a common sewer being in the immediate vicinity. The captain of the ship ascribes it to the rotten condition of the hulk, and to heat generated during the night by so many men being closely packed together, a ward having from ten to twenty-four men sleeping in it, according to its size. The last two cases were of athletic young men, and lasted four days. The former patient was pulseless from the first, and comatose during four hours previous to death—the latter was sensible to the last. They were carefully attended to, and visited every hour, night and day ; and were treated with mercury, mustard poultices, stimulants, and all the usual remedies. The whole of the convicts were removed on the 20th inst. from the *Justitia,* and put on board the *Hebe* and *Sulphur* receiving vessels, opposite the Royal Dockyard ; which arrangement, I find, has created some alarm in the yard.

What Should be Done, if Attacked by Cholera ?

As the great depression of the vital powers, and the consequent coldness of the surface, are the most formidable and striking symptoms, it is obvious that to rouse the system, and restore the warmth of the surface of the body, or, in other words, excite reaction and bring back the circulation of the blood to a natural state, are the objects that require to be effected. A vapour, or Hot Air-bath, should be had recourse to if at hand ; as this, however, will probably but seldom be the case, put the patient into a hot bed, and apply a large hot mustard-poultice over the pit of the stomach. Then let a blanket wrung out of a tub-full of boiling water, as *hot and dry* as possible, be laid over his body, and confine in the vapour, by placing dry blankets over it, renewing it the moment it loses its heat. Put bottles or bladders of hot-water, bags of hot sand, or hot bricks or tiles wrapped in flannel, to his feet ; at the same time rub the feet, legs, and arms with hot flannels. Give the patient a glassful of hot brandy-and-water ; or a tea-spoonful of sal-volatile, or of hartshorn, or of spirits of turpentine, in a glassful of water ; or a tea-spoonful of sulphuric ether in a wine-glass full of camphor julep ; if neither of these liquids be in the house, give hot coffee or tea until some of the above-mentioned remedies can be obtained. If there be much pain in the stomach, or the spasms be severe, or either of the above remedies do not afford relief, give a tea-spoonful, or from 60 to 80 drops of laudanum in the hot brandy-and-water : if there be a severe burning sensation in the stomach, the laudanum should be the first remedy. If the liquid given be rejected, repeat the dose in a few minutes ; and if one remedy will not keep down, try another. Persist in these means till you find the warmth of the skin restored, and the cramps and spasms relieved ; but in the meantime send for a medical person, who will find, on his arrival, half the danger

removed, if you have diligently employed the plan here recommended. Do not fear catching the complaint yourself ; let not that selfish feeling one moment enter your head ; your very exertions will be the best and surest means of preventing your being attacked.—*From " Five Minutes Common Sense about the Asiatic Cholera." By a Fellow of the Royal College of Surgeons of England.*

Where 1 in 2 Babies Died
Illustrated London News, 17 January.

A public meeting was held on Tuesday night " to petition Parliament for a sound and comprehensive sanatory bill, embracing the whole of the metropolis." The attendance was numerous. Mr. Mackinnon, M.P., in opening the proceedings, remarked, that there were five requisites to a healthy habitation ; viz. pure air, a sufficient supply of good water, a perfect drainage, the absence of animal or vegetable putrid matter lying within a certain distance, and that there should be no stagnant water or cesspool within say 200 yards of the dwelling. In 99 cases out of every 100, in the closely inhabited parts of this metropolis, these requisites were not to be found. Then, was it not disgraceful to humanity that a sanatory bill for London should be opposed by any human being ? (Hear, hear.) Yet interested individuals, who apprehended that they would lose something by such a measure, opposed its extension to the City, which of all places in the world most imperiously demanded sanatory measures ! When he had spoken to Lord J. Russell and other members of the Government on the importance of ameliorating the sanatory condition of the population of London, they had answered that they should be happy to do so, but were not able to overcome the opposition of the City (hear, hear) ; not of the people of the City, but the " great dons " who had influence. (Hear, hear.) For instance, from Smith-field market—that still uncorrected abomination—the City derived an enormous revenue. (Hear, hear.) It had

Drouet's notorious "Baby farm" at Tooting, where 180 children died of cholera.

Illustrated London News

been calculated by a very intelligent person then present, that if proper sanatory regulations were adopted in the metropolis, including the metropolitan boroughs, the number of deaths would be diminished by 38 a day. (Hear, hear.) The Legislature, however, would not be deaf to public opinion, respectfully but firmly and steadily expressed. (Hear.)—Dr. Gavin reminded the meeting that in every year, through the neglect of proper sanatory regulations, there occurred in England and Wales 35,000 deaths and 980,000 cases of sickness ; and in London alone 13,800 deaths, and 380,000 cases of sickness. Numbers of children were born only to die from the same cause : in the country, the proportion of children dying under five years of age was 221 in 1000 ; in towns generally, 385 in 1000 ; in Bethnal-green, 479 in 1000. He described the filthy condition of houses in Crown-court, Fleet-street, and the poisonous emanations generated in such spots. No wonder that people who lived in such places were anarchists ; they ought not to be contented with their position. (Hear, hear.) Here must be easy dupes for Chartism, or any delusion that promised an amendment of their condition. (Hear.)—A petition to the Legislature in conformity with the objects of the meeting was then agreed to, and the meeting separated.

Graveyards Scandal

Not only the living but the dead too were overcrowded—and there was no control over how (or where) the latter were buried. Often the two were in unhealthily close proximity. Protests mounted.

Britannia, 22 January and Health of Towns Journal, 2 December.

A public meeting in favour of sanitary reform was held on Wednesday evening at the Hanover-square Rooms. Mr. G. Walker moved:

" That the practice of burying the dead in places surrounded by the abodes of the living has been attended by a disregard of Christian decency, and a violation of the sanctity of the grave. That the frequent exhumation of human remains has engendered a feeling of disrepect for the dead, whilst the constant disturbance of earth, saturated with the decomposing gases emanating from the dead, is seriously destructive of the public health, and should be prohibited by law."

Mr. Walker enforced the adoption of the resolution, by recapitulating the horrible scenes which had come under his notice at Spafields burying-ground, at Enon Chapel, and elsewhere and assuring the meeting that there were still in London infinite

Spafields burying-grounds and Enon Chapels, diffusing disease and death around.

Compared with these pestilential depositaries, the metropolitan grave-yards, the evil of slaughter-houses, knacker-yards, and other nuisances, is but small. The existence of such abominations in populous places is inveighed against with unanswerable reason, but it is truly surprising that the continued interment of human bodies is tacitly permitted, thousands of carcases being unceasingly laid down, many of them but slightly covered, in crowded thoroughfares, close to the walls, by the doors, and under the windows of thickly surrounding houses. Not only must the apartments of these dwellings be filled with the grave-yard effluvia, but in hot weather the foetid air is wafted through the atmosphere ; and when the great number of burial-grounds, within the metropolis, overteeming with mortal remains, and notwithstanding the extensive cemeteries now laid out in distant suburbs, still the receptacle of putrefying masses is taken into consideration, it may enable one to form an idea of the magnitude of the barbarous practice.

The Golgotha at Enon Chapel

Weekly Times, 5 March.

Arrangements for entirely removing the remains of mortality from this notorious burying-place, having been for some time in progress, we visited it for the first time on Saturday. It is altogether impossible to describe by any language whatever, or to convey by the use of words the mingled sensations of surprise, disgust, and horror which were excited in us by the first glance of this abominable golgotha. All that we had read of its impurities, its atrocities, and its pollution, had failed to produce any distinct impression of the horrible reality, which must be seen to be believed or thoroughly comprehended. The whole coffins, which were found in the cellar (for it is nothing else), under the floor of the chapel, have been brought up, and in many cases filled with skulls and human bones, for the convenience of transporting them elsewhere. These coffins, and others not broken open, occupy a large portion of the floor. The upper end is covered with a mass of broken-up coffins, and one side of the building presents a huge pile of human bones—in some cases skulls with the flesh still adhering to the scalp. The sight is truly sickening. But the horror felt by the spectator at the mere sight of these remains of mortality is dispersed when he is informed that the largest half of that huge pile of bones has been raised from under the flag-stones which paved the cellar under the kitchen of the late proprietor of this pestiferous nuisance. We descended to the place from which they had been excavated, in layers several feet deep. It was evident that, after getting rid of the soft parts of the body, by means of quicklime and other more atrocious means, the bones were pitched wholesale through an opening in the brick wall, which separates the small cellar under the large cellar, under what was termed a chapel, for the purpose of concealing from the public the manufacture of disease upon a large scale. In the larger cellar, which we also examined, workmen were busy excavating another mass of human bones, and the *debris* of bodies from behind a sewer which runs obliquely through it ; from the quantity thrown out it would appear that a very large addition will be made to the mass already collected above. The place has evidently been expressly constructed for carrying on this dreadful trade. On the only side from which it can be overlooked ingenious contrivances were resorted to, to give a somewhat decent exterior, while the side of the chapel, next to Clement's Inn, is built upon arches and separated a few inches from the wall of the Inn, thus providing for the escape of at least a part of the deadly generated filth in this wholesale manufactory of disease and death. It was not alone the poor inhabitants of dirty, crowded, ill-ventilated St. Clement's-lane who were poisoned by it, but the respectable professional residents of Clement's Inn, who little dreamt the air they inhaled was constantly impregnated with gases as fatal to life as a more tangible dose of arsenic. The body of the proprietor of this detestable place has been discovered during these exhumations. It is recognised by the peculiar lameness of the left foot, and in consequence of having een, like many other of the bodies nterred here, sprinkled with quick-lime, is a perfect mummy. The hair still adheres in some places to the head, and the whiskers to the face ! One or two other bodies similarly mummified are also in the chapel, proving clearly the nature of the modes which were had recourse to, in order to dispose rapidly of the remains of those brought here for interment, and make room for more.

A Sanitary Song
Builder, 1 January.

Close your eyelids and fold your arms
    Good easy people about,
In filth and stench, from sewer and trench,
    Have your nap securely out.
Cram your dead into recking vaults,
    As herrings are crammed in barrels,
Then cheek by jowl, with the dead men
                    foul,
Go on with your loves and your
                    quarrels.

Only—a plague may be coming ;
    Only—beware of the knells
Which a livid grisly phantom
    May ring on your own door bells.

Putting Sewage to Good Use

In an age when the understanding of agricultural chemistry had leapt ahead, even amateur scientists recognized that sewage should not be allowed to go to waste.

Weekly Chronicle, 8 January and 4 March.

At a time when the importance of an efficient drainage of London is urged, the sentiments expressed by Mr. Heyworth, a Liverpool merchant, in a letter addressed by him to the Health of Towns Association, may be considered highly interesting. Mr. Heyworth says,—By means of earthen pipes, small covered cesspools, and stench trays, I convey all the waste water, including that from the water closets, chambers, scullery, washhouse,

&c., and all other feculent matter in a diluted state, from my residence, stables, sheep pens, &c., into one end of a large excavated dungpit, which, being always covered with litter, never allows any escape of noxious effluvia ; at the other end of the pit I have a covered well outside, communicating by small openings with the bottom of this pit, from which the fluid manure is lifted by a pump into a covered water tight cart, and carried upon the fields. The quantity of this liquid manure from my single establishment covers annually about 20 acres, and renders them profusely luxuriant. For the rainwater and springs I have separate and distinct drains, which is an essential arrangement. What should prevent a scheme so encouragingly profitable from being applied in collecting and distributing the liquid manure of towns generally.

———

When the proposed sanitary plans have been put into thorough operation, we may look to have the whole of agricultural England permeated with sewage mains and pipes for the distribution of sewage water over the surface. The experiment will be

Selling water was profitable where no mains supply existed.

first tried in the vicinity of London, by a public company. Pipes will be laid down from the London sewers to the country around Hounslow. The pipes will be arranged at convenient distances, and have openings, to which hose may be fitted, and by the hose the sewage water will be thrown over the fields. In the district to which the sewage will first be directed in this experiment, the appetite of the farmers and cultivators is already sharpened, and they are ready to take and pay for all that can be conveyed to them ; they are only afraid the supply will not be sufficient. The system of sewage supply will doubtless go on until the country, for many miles round London, is ramified with sewage pipes, and the soil as regularly supplied with manure as the streets of the city with water or gas. Then we may look for its general extension into the country. Such a diffuse and extensive network of pipage cannot but startle the reader at the first thought, but, in this age, it is not for us to be surprised, and to doubt the triumphs of mechanical skill, however extensive the new trial of its power may be. We who have seen gas extend itself to every city and town in the kingdom, who have seen " the ringing grooves of change " replace the old travelling roads, and the electric telegraph do the work of the old and cumbrous signals ; who have seen extensive districts drained for agricultural purposes in the most scientific manner ; it is not for us, with all these circulations in full and beneficial play, to doubt that the sewage circulation will come into successful work, until every field and garden has its system, both drainage and supply.

Uncommon Sausages

Adulteration of foodstuffs was commonplace. So was lack of hygiene in their preparation. With no system of food inspection, there was little control over the quality or fitness for food.

Britannia, 8 January.

Mordecai Andrews, a countryman, was brought before Mr. Tyrwhitt, at the Clerkenwell Police Court, on Monday charged by a City constable with having in his possession meat unfit for human food

At an early hour in the morning the prisoner was observed near Smithfield with a horse and cart, the latter containing two dead cows and a horse, and the most offensive effluvium proceeded from them The policeman, suspecting that they were meant for sausage-meat, followed the prisoner until he arrived at the premises of Mr. Lansdowne, a sausage-merchant, of Sharpe's-alley, Cow-cross, where he backed the cart in, but Mr. Lansdowne told the party that it was a mistake, and the carcases were not meant for him. The officer, knowing that the dead carcases were not fit for human diet, questioned the prisoner, who hesitated, and gave such an unsatisfactory account of his possession of the animals, that he took him and the property to the nearest station-house.

Inspector Julian, G, and the City officer, stated that there were many dead carcases in Mr. Lansdowne's yard.

Mr. John Atcheler was sworn, and said he was horse-slaughterer to her Majesty and the Royal Family, and he resided in Sharpe's-square, Cow-cross, Smithfield—(A laugh). He had no knowledge of the prisoner, and was satisfied in his own mind that the carcases were consigned to his establishment, which was well watered, and kept as sweet as any lady's drawing-room—(Laughter). His neighbour, Mr. Lansdowne, was a respectable man, and did not make the common sausages, but only those that were fit for the west end of the town—(Much laughter). He meant the real German sausages, which were of the very best meat, mixed with a bit of " tommy."

Mr. Mould (the clerk) : Do you mean Tommy Cat ?

Mr. Atcheler : Oh ! no ; a little of bull beef, which makes them good and stiff, and more palatable—what Lord Brougham likes—(Laughter). He added, that how the prisoner could have been entrusted with the care of a horse and cart and such goods was to him a puzzle, for he was as green as a leek.

Mr. Josiah Knight, veterinary surgeon, of St. Andrew's hill, Doctors' commons, deposed that the animals were not fit for human food. They had died from disease, and had undergone medical treatment.

Mr. Tyrwhitt : Would they be dangerous to the health if they were eaten as human food ?—Witness : I can't say that ; but any person of experience must know that they were not fit for human food.

Mr. Tyrwhitt : Do they make sausages of such carcases ?—Witness : I cannot say.

Mr. Tyrwhitt : I can only say that parties on whose premises such carcases are found are liable to indictment.

Mr. Atcheler : I can only say, your worship, that, if they boils 'em in my coppers, we are always obliged to put a little bull into it, to make it sound and good, and stiff, too, for the canines—(Laughter).

Mr. Tyrwhitt said that he could not punish the prisoner, who was the instrument of some person who cared little about the health of the public as long as he could make money. He asked the prisoner who employed him to bring the carcases to London ?—Prisoner : Mr. Henry Parish, of Bishop's Stortford.

Mr. Tyrwhitt said he must discharge the prisoner, but it was a matter of great importance at this period, when disease was caused through nauseous smells and vapours, and such proceedings ought to be carefully watched.

Houses Without Daylight

Most hated of all taxes was the one on windows. It was so onerous that many windows were bricked in so as to escape the tax. In every city, there was increasing pressure to get it removed, but the government would not yield.

Weekly Times, 13 February, and Carmarthen Journal, 17 November.

A meeting of ratepayers of the parish of St. James, Westminster, was held at the Crown Tavern, for the purpose of taking measures to procure the Total Repeal of the Window-tax.—Mr. Niven proposed the first resolution, which was to the effect that a petition be presented to Parliament for a Total Repeal of the Window-tax, without which no sanitary measure was complete. He proceeded to give a general review of the gradual growth of that tax, from its origin in the house tax of the reign of William III, to its establishment in its present form, and gradual increase by William Pitt, to which Minister, however, it was a popular delusion to ascribe the whole of the odium attached to its introduction. A great portion of the deficiency which it would cause in the revenue would be covered by the extra amount of glass, wood, lead, and paint—all articles paying duty—which would be consumed in consequence—in addition to which, the extra employment which would be given to a large number of persons was a material point. Some years ago Lord Althorp had promised that the tax should be repealed, and, in consequence, a large number of windows in the parish, which had previously been shut up, were opened. Some time after this a new survey was made, and every window so opened was charged with the duty. Mr. Austin seconded the resolution. He was surprised that in the report of the sanitary commission there had been no allusion to the window-tax, which he considered to be a material point of the subject. Those commissioners had requested the authorities of St. James, Westminster, to make an examination into the state of the poorer habitations in that parish. The returns made showed that there were 1150 habitations on the ground, which were unfit for human abode. He considered that that fact ought to have given the commissioners an idea as to the evils of the tax. Out of 3,500,000 houses in Great Britain not more than 500,000 were chargeable with the window-tax. There was no doubt that many gentlemen's houses escaped, because they were classed as warehouses, or were in the occupation of gentlemen farmers, or were exempt from other causes—so that a very small part of the sum paid was contributed to by the rich, the great burden falling upon the lower classes. The resolution was carried unanimously, and a large number of signatures affixed to the petition.

An iron grating over a coal-hole, unless wholly closed to exclude light, has been decided by the Judges to be chargeable as a window.

An Ideal Home ?

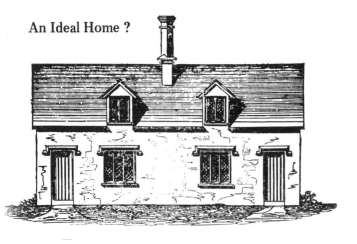

GROUND FLOOR PLAN.

UPPER FLOOR PLAN.

Illustrated London News, 3 June.

The prevailing squalor prompted the Society for Improving the Condition of the Labouring Classes (president, Prince Albert) to publish plans for model houses for workers. Modest though they were (no bath or w.c.), few ever got built.

Weekly Times, 30 July

You seek the home of taste, and find
    The proud mechanic there,—
Rich as a king, and less a slave,
    Throned on his elbow chair ;
Or on his sofa reading Locke
    Beside his open door ;
Why start ? why envy worth like his ?
    The carpet on his floor ?

You seek the home of sluttery—
    " Is John at home ?" you say ;
" No, sir, he's at the Sportsman's Arms,
    The dog-fights o'er the way."
Oh, lift the workman's heart and mind
    Above low sensual sin ;
Give him a home—the home of taste—
    Outbid the house of sin !

Ebenezer Eliot

Below and right : slums like these were normal (St. Giles and Duke Street, Southwark, in London).

Chloroform in the News

Weekly Times, 2 and 13 January and Bradford Observer.

An operation in surgery, of a very formidable and intricate nature, was performed on Monday last, by Mr. Thomas Wakley, at the Royal Free Hospital. The chloroform was used on the occasion with complete success. There were between thirty and forty practitioners present, who appeared to view the operation with great interest, as it was the first time that it had ever been performed. The operation consisted in dissecting out the two chief bones of the foot, and in cutting off the ends of the bones of the leg which form the inner and outer ankles. The bones were dissected out in less than six minutes, and the remaining portion of the foot having been adjusted in its new position by a

---

Chloroform had only just been recognized as an anaesthetic, and the first operations without the patient conscious were regularly reported in the press. Anaesthesia made it possible for more complicated operations to be performed. Childbirth was eased. Deaths after operations dropped sharply.

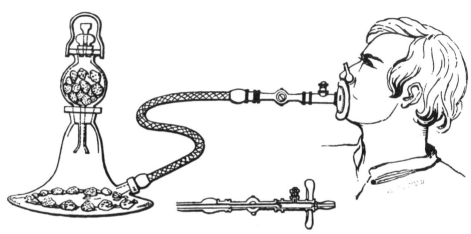

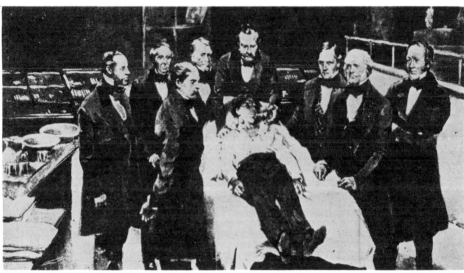

bandage, the patient was removed to his bed, where he expressed his gratitude to the operator, and declared that he had not felt the slightest pain.

Mrs. Goodman, having fallen down a flight of stairs, and being within a few days of her expected confinement with her twelfth child, some apprehension was felt lest the accident might be productive of mischievous results, especially as on all previous occasions the crisis of parturition had been peculiarly painful. Mrs. Goodman, having read in the newspapers statements of the salutary influence of chloroform, expressed her wish to try its effects. Mr. Alford (surgeon-accoucheur) yielded to the entreaty, and applied on a handkerchief, which she held to her nostrils, some drops of the fluid. The patient gently resigned herself to a sound sleep, and to her infinite delight and astonishment, on awaking about half-past 4, was informed that she had been safely delivered of a healthy boy.

Quack Remedies

There was no control over false claims in advertising, nor over the composition of medicines.

Health of Towns Journal, 18 November.

The suppression of the advertisements of quacks is an object well worthy of the consideration of those whose duty it is to promote the public health. It is most desirable that these dealers in poisons should be indicted for endangering the health and lives of her Majesty's subjects. It is impossible to peruse the unqualified recommendations of quack medicines, rife throughout the streets of London and the pages of the periodical press, and to reflect how many simple and unsuspecting persons may be deceived by them, without fearing that much evil may arise from this nuisance, should cholera actually come amongst us. Can the authorities really be in earnest in their endeavours to promote the health of the people, when they permit the display of placards with such announcements as these—" Infallible Prevention of Cholera !" " Certain Cure for Cholera !"

applied to the nostrums of notorious and unscrupulous quacks !

Illustrated London News advertisements

The Insane Unchained

A more enlightened attitude towards mental illness was just beginning.

Illustrated London News, 15 January.

" Seven years have elapsed since the experiment of non-restraint has been fully tried in the Hanwell Asylum ; and Dr. Conolly, in the spirit of a Christian philosopher, thanks God, with deep and unfeigned humility, that nothing has occurred during that period to throw discredit on the great principle for which he has so ably battled."

We quote this emphatic testimony of the success of the non-restraint system of management of Lunatic Asylums from the first Number of the *Journal of Psychological Medicine and Mental Pathology*, edited by Dr. Forbes Winslow ; a work specially devoted to the humane treatment of the Insane and from which the most beneficial results may be anticipated.

The accompanying Engraving presents a very interesting illustration of the non-restraint system pursued at Hanwell. Among the in-door recreations for the patients during the winter days and evenings, music is the greatest favourite.

The patients often have small parties for dancing, and there are some entertainments on a larger scale. On the 6th instant the usual Twelfth Night entertainment was given to the male patients.

BELOW THE POVERTY LINE

The good neighbourliness of village life had once, to some extent, looked after the sick, the destitute, the orphans and the handicapped. But now the urban poor (10% of the population) had to fend for themselves—there was no concept of social security to help them. Public concern expressed itself only through private charity : inadequate, often humiliating, and usually conditional upon the good behaviour and piety of the deserving poor who received it. In the workhouses, shelter of the starkest kind was given in exchange for work on the premises. Conditions were deliberately made disagreeable to discourage applicants, and husbands were often separated from wives to prevent the birth of further paupers.

Perishing Outside the Workhouse

Times.

Last evening, a numerous and very stormy meeting took place at the Assembly-rooms, Theobald's-road, Mr. C. Cochrane in the chair, to take into consideration, as the requisition stated, " the disgusting and immoral practices, sanctioned and encouraged by the guardians of several metropolitan unions, of allowing the male inmates of the casual wards to sleep together in a state of nudity."

The Chairman, in opening the proceedings, distributed some copies of a publication called " The Poor Man's Guardian," containing a woodcut representing the interior of the casual wards in the Holborn, St. Martin's, and West London unions, showing the occupants sleeping in the manner described.

Mr. White, surgeon of the Holborn Union, here rose, and, amidst considerable uproar, proceeded to address the meeting. He emphatically denied that the casual ward of the Holborn Union was kept in a filthy state. The board of guardians did not sanction the disgusting practice complained of. But could the commissioners find shirts for the number of casual poor who resorted to the workhouse nightly ? They complained also of the poor people perishing and lying outside the doors, and, at the same time, of the wards being crowded. To avoid the one evil they must incur the other. The increase of the number of poor was very great, and the workhouse had been like an hospital for the last six months. The speaker ultimately left the room, being unable to obtain a hearing.

The second resolution was then put and carried. It was as follows :—" That the Poor Law, as at present constituted, is harsh and cruel towards the poor in some of its enactments, but that the law is rendered much more obnoxious by the unfeeling and disgraceful manner in which it is administered by many of the boards of guardians and or oppression."

It was then moved and carried that a petition should be entrusted to Mr. Wakley to present to Parliament.

Inside a Workhouse

Weekly Times (reader's letter),
20 February.

Sir,—After correspondence had taken place with the governors and directors of the poor of St. Margaret's and St. John's workhouse, Westminster, I was, on Monday, permitted, at half-past twelve o'clock, to examine the internal arrangements of this establishment. The first department we entered was the kitchen, pantry, &c. They were very small and dark, and had a close and very unpleasant smell. I observed to the cook, that her dresser, on which she chopped up her meat, was not quite so clean as could be desired, as the surface was besmeared with fat, which also filled up the spaces made by the chopper. She replied that it was difficult to keep it cleaner, unless the boards were planed down a little, and the lodgments for the grease removed. There was a very good supply of meat in the larder, and of the two soups which I tasted, I found the pea-soup very good, although I cannot speak quite so favourably of the broth, which formed the dinner meal of the day, and I rather think the supply of bread allowed was somewhat scanty. We then proceeded to the ward for infants, and on our way entered the bath-rooms, containing a bath for the inmates ; but as is the case generally in workhouses, although it is always stated the poor have baths when required, it is very difficult to learn how often the baths are made use of. On the ground-floor, was a flagged pavement, in a very wet state, in consequence of the water which ran to waste, from a cistern close by. Beside this cistern, was a water-closet for the children ; but from its wet and damp state, arising from leakage, was hardly, I think, in a safe or fit condition for use. The arrangement for the ablution of the boys consisted of a large tub, placed on the flag stones referred to, in which they washed themselves, about four or five at a time. After visiting an adjoining room, devoted to religious worship, we proceeded to inspect various female wards. The inmates were chiefly old persons ; and in ward No. 36, there were 21 invalid or infirm persons, and in No. 37 there were 20. There the poor slept *two in a bed,* and considering that the beds were very close together, the rooms very low, and the means of ventilation very imperfect, I fear the curative process must be very slow. In No. 35 there were 13 invalids, very much crowded together, and I found a young woman suffering under syphilitic disease, lying in a bed over which was hanging wet linen to dry, and the nurse, when spoken to on the subject, did not appear to consider this as likely to prejudice the health of the patient. On inquiring of her as to the number of towels the *thirteen invalids* had allowed them, she informed me *one* round or jack towel, *changed once a week.* In ward 52, there were twenty-two beds, in each of which two men slept together, and two single beds and two others placed on the floor for want of bedsteads—so that the whole of the space was entirely occupied, to the serious prejudice, I should think, to the health of the inmates from overcrowding. There was one round towel, the nurse informed me, changed once a week, for about twelve or thirteen persons, and the men who were so invalided as to be unable to go down stairs, washed themselves in pails placed at the corner of a landing-place on the stairs. I now examined the washing-places and necessaries for the men in the yard. The arrangements of the former were very rough, and the latter very bad. The smell coming from them was offensive, and in one case the drainage into the sewer was completely impeded, and accumulations of dirty water in the yard were in consequence created.

I was informed that the girls, who generally learnt to read and write well, are put out to service at the age of 13. I was sorry to hear this, as, from the information which I have obtained of the fate which generally attends workhouse children so employed, I fear their career is of a description which the friends of morality could not desire.

I now examined the washing places and necessaries allotted to the women. The former consisted of sinks and one or two wooden bowls, beside a cistern, and the latter of the ordinary description, one-half of which was covered with wet. The yard and necessary had a stone pavement, which was also very damp and wet, and could not fail to cause the poor women to get their feet wet when standing on it. At the end of

this yard, or court, was the oakum-room, in which I found a large number of women chiefly advanced in years. This room was formerly the dead-house, and the poor women complained very much of its dampness, causing them severe rheumatics ; one side of the room was perfectly wet from water which leaked from a drain connected as I was informed with a water-closet, and which, at times, produced a most intolerable smell. I observed one poor creature sitting in her pattens to keep off the damp. It certainly struck me as an unfit place for women to remain in, particularly when infirm or old. After visiting some more wards for females, wherein I remarked night-stools were used in lieu of water closets, we went over to the fever ward, which is detached from the principal building. This, as I have already stated, was a casual ward, but from want of room, is converted to its present purpose. The room was very dark, and badly ventilated, and contained about five or six patients.

I beg further to add, for the information of the Governors and Directors of the Poor, that on my leaving this establishment I went to the hospital close by, being aware there was space within sufficient to admit of sixty beds, but which space was either occupied as store-rooms or else to no purpose whatever, or, in other words, thrown away from want of funds. I had an earnest conversation with the enlightened and benevolent secretary on the subject, and I cannot but feel that if the governors will devote a reasonable amount of money for the better protection of their sick poor, they would be enabled to ensure them an early admission into this splendid hospital, and, I think I may add, an early cure, and thereby obtain more room for the remainder of the inmates, who now look up to them for protection and support in their poverty and old age.—I remain, Mr. Editor, your obedient humble Servant, CHARLES COCHRANE, Poor Man's Guardian Society

The Guardians of the Poor

Weekly Times (reader's letter),
20 February.

Sir,—The Poor-law has been found to be *bad* in *theory and in practice.* But, bad as the law is, the administration of it is worse. The unkindness, nay more, the cruel harshness shown to the poor—the guilty and guiltless alike, by the dispensers of the law, and countenanced by the Guardians of the Poor, makes the latter hate the asylums which the country has provided for them in their distress. The poor man goes to the Guardians, and expects in his distress to find a friend and a protector ; but the Guardians treats all the poor as though they were criminals, without taking the trouble, as he should do, to inquire into the circumstances and character of any applicant. This is his duty, and he should understand that if there is any honour attached to the office, there is also great responsibility ; in fact, there is often life and death in his power. The poor creature whose application has been neglected and spurned has perhaps in a few hours

furnished a paragraph for a newspaper, and "death from starvation" is all that remains to tell the tale of previous suffering on the one hand, and official neglect on the other. There is no office in the whole range of our law, or of our institutions, on which devolves so much responsibility and care as the office of Poor-law Guardian. They should be men of

In the workhouses, sexes were strictly segregated.

great humanity and discretion, a happy mixture of economy and patience, just, without being generous, and they should have ample time to devote to their duties.

But what a picture does the guardian at present represent—selfishness and neglect are his attributes ; a kind of dogged indifference to public opinion predominates in him. The whole of his duty, as guardian, he imagines to consist of maintaining all who become paupers at as minimum a cost as possible. How, Sir, under such circumstances can you expect our "institutions to become more charitable ?" We have, first, a bad law ; and secondly, a bad administration of the law.

About 400 able-bodied men could be employed in cleansing the streets of the metropolis above the number now so occupied. We have demonstrated this fact theoretically and practically to almost every parish in the metropolis. It has been also shown that it would be reproductive employment, that it would prove a saving to the ratepayers. But how have these efforts been met by the various boards of guardians ? If we go to them, they say, " Oh ! we have nothing to do with the cleansing of the streets ; go to the paving boards." We go to the paving boards, and the answer is, " We have nothing to do with the employment of the poor ; go to the guardians," and so a question involving the social comfort of two millions of inhabitants, and the employment of thousands of unemployed poor is knocked about by two sets of men, as though they were playing a game of battledore and shuttlecock.

I have the honour to be, Sir, your obedient servant, M. DAVIES, Secretary to the National Philanthropic Association.

The Guardians' Instructions

The Guardians administering the Poor Law and the workhouses were elected annually. New regulations were issued to them at the beginning of the year in an attempt to improve the paupers' treatment.

Weekly Times, 2 January.

On the pauper's admission he is to be searched, and all articles prohibited by any Act of Parliament or by this order, which may be found on his person, shall be taken from him and, so far as may be proper, restored to him at his departure from the workhouse.

The paupers, as far as the workhouse admits, are to be classed as follows :—Class 1. Men infirm through age or any other cause. Class 2. Able-bodied men and youths above 15 years. Class 3. Boys above the age of 7 years and under that of 15. Class 4. Women infirm through age or any other cause. Class 5. Able-bodied women and girls above the age of 15 years. Class 6. Girls above the age of 7 years and under that of 15. Class 7. Children under 7 years of age. To each class shall be assigned that ward or separate building and yard which may be best fitted for the reception of such class, and each class of paupers shall remain therein without communication with those of any other class.

The guardians shall, so far as circumstances permit, further subdivide any of the class enumerated with reference to the moral character or behaviour, or the previous habits of the inmates, or to such other grounds as may seem expedient. That nothing in this order shall compel the guardians to separate any married couple, being both paupers of the first and fourth classes respectively, provided the guardians shall set apart for the exclusive use of every such couple a sleeping apartment separate from that of the other paupers. The master (subjected to any directions given or regulations made by the guardians) shall allow the father or mother of any child in the same workhouse who may be desirous of seeing such child to have an interview with such child at some one time in each day, in the said workhouse, and should there be more than one workhouse in the parish, and the members of the same family are separated, they are to have occasional interviews with each.

The casual poor wayfarers are to be kept in a separate ward, and to be dieted and set to work under regulations of the guardians. No pauper of unsound mind is to be kept in the workhouse for any period exceeding fourteen days, and to be removed to some asylum or licensed house as soon as practicable.

The paupers belonging to the 2d, 3d, 5th and 6th classes are, from the 25th of March to the 29th of September, to rise at a quarter before six, and to go to bed at eight o'clock. They are to work for ten hours, and the remainder time is to be divided for the breakfast, dinner, and supper ; the other period of the year they are to rise one hour later. No two paupers above the age of seven years are to occupy the same bed, unless in the case of a mother and infant children ; and that they are to be kept employed according to their capacity and ability ; but the boys and girls who are inmates of the workhouse shall, for three of the working hours at least every day, be instructed in reading, writing, arithmetic, and the principles of the Christian religion, and such other instruction shall be imparted to them as may fit them for service, and train them to habits of usefulness, industry, and virtue. No written or printed paper of an improper tendency, or which may be likely to produce insubordination, shall be allowed to circulate or be read out among the inmates of the workhouse. No game of chance, or cards, or smoking, be permitted ; and that no work, except the necessary household work and cooking, shall be performed by the paupers on Sunday, Good Friday, and Christmas-day. In the case of disorderly paupers and which are enumerated, the master, without the intervention of the guardians, can punish, by substituting for a period not greater than forty-eight hours, for his dinner, eight ounces of bread or one pound of cooked potatoes, or boiled rice, and by withholding for the same period all butter, cheese, tea, sugar, or broth, which he would otherwise receive, while the guardians may, by a special direction, punish any refractory pauper by confinement, for a period not exceeding twenty-four hours, with or without an alteration of his diet. No pauper shall be confined between eight o'clock in the evening and six o'clock in the morning, without being furnished with a bed, clothing, &c., suitable to the season. That no child under twelve years of age shall be punished by confinement in a dark room during the night. No corporal punishment shall be inflicted on any male child, except by the schoolmaster or master ; no corporal punishment shall be inflicted on any female child, the article to be used in the punishment to be a rod, unless ordered otherwise by the guardians ; and before the punishment is awarded two hours are to elapse from the commission of the offence ; while those who are above the age of fourteen years are to be exempt from flogging. In all cases of paupers punished without the direction of the guardians, the offence and punishment to be entered in a book, and which book is to be laid on the table at each meeting of the guardians. Should the board consider the punishment to have been improper or illegal the case to be forwarded to the commissioners, while the punished pauper can come before the board, if he or she wishes.

Last refuge for the destitute ; inside a hated workhouse.

The Ragged Schools

Illustrated London News and Family Herald, 8 January and 24 June.

On Tuesday, the children of the Lamb-and-Flag Ragged Schools, to the number of near two hundred, were regaled with a substantial entertainment of roast beef and plum pudding, bread and potatoes.

On Wednesday afternoon the second annual meeting of the friends and supporters of the Ragged School in Marylebone was attended by a large number of the neighbouring gentry. Lord Ashley, M.P., took the chair, and said he had no doubt whatever that ragged schools would soon receive Government aid. (Hear, hear.) From what had passed in the House of Commons, and from private communications he had had with Government, he knew that a certain number of those poor, destitute, and helpless children who had obtained certificates of good conduct at the schools, and were qualified by a certain amount of education, would be transplanted to a soil where they might industriously, honestly, and happily pass the remainder of their days. (Hear, hear.) Sir George Grey, the Colonial Secretary, said to him (Lord Ashley) a few days ago, " If you take care to attend to the moral training of those children, imbue them with religious principles, and give them a knowledge of some industrial occupation so as to fit them for labour, then I do not hesitate to assert that the means at the disposal of Government will be employed to convey them to the British possessions abroad."

Last week Lord Ashley laid before the House of Commons an immense quantity of facts, grouped statistically or in dramatic detail, concerning the habits and pursuits—the natural history, as he called it—of the class for whom he spoke. He commenced with 2,345 names on the books of fifteen particular Ragged Schools ; the average attendance in which was about 1,600. Of these, 162 had often been in prison ; 253 lived chiefly by begging ; 216 had neither shoes nor stockings ; 280 no cap, hat, or bonnet ; 101 no scrap of body linen ; 249 had no recollection of having ever slept in a bed ; 68 were children of convicts, 125 of stepmothers, 306 orphans. The average attendance on the schools was some 4,000 : the proportions above, if applied to this number, gave 660 who lived by begging, 178 children of convicts, and 800 orphans. Glancing at their occupations as street sweepers, match-sellers, holders of horses, and agents of dealers in marine stores—in other words, boys on the staff of receivers of stolen goods—he indicated the mode in which they passed their nights—under bridges, viaducts, door-ways, in saw-pits, lime-kilns, and empty vehicles, in the open air, on the bare earth. One, with whom Lord Ashley had spoken personally, slept through the inclement winter of last year in the great iron roller in the Regent's park ; this boy had a friend, another boy who was even worse off than himself ; and to this boy he went one day, and said, " Come along with me, and I'll let you into a good thing :" he brought his friend to the iron roller and the two boys slept there together for the remainder of the winter. In the " parlour " of one of the lodging-houses, measuring 18 feet by 10, were shavings made up for no less than 27 male and female adults, and 31 children, who slept promiscuously each night—with several dogs in addition.

Soup Kitchens

The Britannia, 15 January and 5 March.

The soup-kitchen now open in Leicester-square presents a remarkable aspect, from the daily assemblage of large numbers of the distressed and destitute who are congregated round the building in order to receive their soup-tickets. A more miserable set of beings can scarcely be met with, and yet among them are usually to be seen some who, though evidently suffering under the most biting poverty, yet show, by their decent exterior and quiet demeanour, that they experience a sense of deep humiliation in their unhappy position. It is impossible to describe the impatience and eagerness evinced by all these unhappy sufferers to obtain from the secretary the soup-ticket. The crowding, from the struggle to be in time, proves clearly the hunger they feel, for they strive

Prince Albert visiting a soup kitchen.   *Illustrated London News*

for the tickets as if they contended for the preservation of their existence. The kitchen where the bread and soup are distributed is large and convenient. Judging from the taste, the soup is of excellent quality, as it is very palatable and comforting. It is gratifying to observe the pleasurable expression gradually imparted to the countenances of these poor creatures as the reviving effect of the nourishment became apparent, as well as to listen to the expressions of gratitude frequently uttered. From the immense number of applicants, however, it is found impossible to relieve all, and, though hundreds are supplied, hundreds are compelled to "go hungry away" with countenances replete with despair.

The Leicester-square soup-kitchen, recently visited by Prince Albert, still continues to afford warm nourishing soup and bread gratuitously to upwards of 800 poor creatures daily. Although the weather is mild for the season, it will not satisfy hunger, and there are thousands wandering about the metropolis in search of work, and actually starving.—"*Deaths from want*" are constantly to be seen recorded in the public newspapers. Poor famishing creatures beset us in every corner of the streets with the cry, " I am perishing from hunger, pray relieve me." This is shocking in a Christian country. We regret to hear that the committee of the institution will soon be compelled to close the soup-kitchen, unless the public support

them more actively ; and when such an event takes place, a thousand poor creatures will have no alternative than to starve, to beg, or to steal. Let the benevolent pause over the fact, that a guinea given to the soup-kitchen will prevent upwards of a hundred persons suffering from want, and " He gives twice who gives quickly."

Classless Destitution
Weekly Times, 16 January.

There are many instances, we are told, of governesses, widows of medical men, military and naval officers, seeking the soup kitchen for temporary relief. Some would bring jugs, requesting permission to take the soup away to be divided among their children at home, and which was always allowed when their representations were known to be correct. The details of the miseries of those who had once been possessed of affluence, were peculiarly distressing. Surgeons, apothecaries, preachers, literary men, tradesmen of all classes, whilst the greater number consist of mechanics, artizans, servants out of place, and labourers in search of work. And, although there are some who belong to an idle, disorderly, and dissolute class, and who are disinclined to labour for their livelihood, they form but a very small amount of the tide of human misery that daily flows towards this soup kitchen as a harbour of refuge.

Soyer's Recipes

The celebrated chef of the Reform Club had a social conscience and practical ideas. He offered the poor more than bread and soup.

Illustrated London News, 26 February.

Soyer's Parochial Model Kitchen has just been opened in Spitalfields, where 10,000 poor reside, with a very small number of wealthy neighbours to assist them. M. Soyer was so impressed with this melancholy fact that he at once caused one of his model kitchens to be set up in the above district, and from it will be distributed beef-soup, peas panada, and rice curry, at the rate of a quart for one penny, with a quarter of a pound of bread. It is proposed to defray the expense of this distribution by public subscription, to be accounted for monthly, showing the cost, ingredients consumed, and number of persons relieved. We hope this philanthropic plan will succeed ; for, judicious economy combined with charitable dispensation, may effect wonders in the relief of public distress.

SOYER'S SAUCE,

Diet of the Poor

How considerable an improvement Soyer's meals were is shown by a more typical recipe for " a good dinner " for paupers—from " The Family Economist. A penny monthly magazine devoted to the moral, physical and domestic improvement of the industrious classes."

Put one pound of rice and one pound of Scotch barley into two gallons of water, and boil them gently for four hours over a slow fire ; then add four ounces of treacle and one ounce of salt, and let the whole simmer for half-an-hour. It will produce *sixteen pounds* of good food.

Sentenced for Starving

Britannia and Weekly Times, 22 and 30 January.

At the Middlesex Sessions, on Tuesday, *John Poole, John Smith, John Barrett, Thomas Williams, James Johnson,* and *Thomas Mills,* were indicted for stealing a loaf of bread value 3½d. The first two pleaded guilty.

The prisoners are " navigators "* out of employment, and on the 13th inst., as they were passing along Marylebone-lane, Poole and Smith entered the shop of the prosecutor and took up a loaf, with which they made off and joined the other prisoners. The prosecutor followed and gave them into custody. The prisoners said they were starving, and that was the reason why they had taken the bread. On their being searched only one halfpenny was found amongst them. They were on the way to the office for the purpose of obtaining tickets for a night's lodging. They had not been in bed or tasted food for eight-and-forty hours.

The judge, in his summing up, said it was dreadful to contemplate that in this great and wealthy metropolis so many unfortunate men should be walking about the streets in a state of starvation, and committing robberies in order to satisfy the cravings of nature. He would take that opportunity of mentioning a very painful

* *Railway navvies.*

case which had come under his notice as one of the visiting justices of the Westminster Bridewell, in which a prisoner who had been committed there for a similar offence had afterwards died. On his admission the prisoner was found to be in such a wretched state of emaciation that it was necessary to place him in the infirmary, where he received every attention that medical skill could devise, but without effect. A coroner's jury sat on the body, and returned a verdict that he died of starvation. The court did not sit to administer justice with a stern and unrelenting hand, but while protecting the rights of property it was their duty to attend to the sufferings of humanity.

The jury returned a verdict of *Guilty* against the prisoners, with a request that the court would deal with them as leniently as possible.

The court sentenced them to one month's imprisonment in the House of Correction.

On Tuesday evening, a meeting was convened at the Western Literary Society, Leicester-square, by the Poor Man's Guardian Society, " to petition her Majesty to pardon John Poole, John Smith, John Barrett, Thomas Williams, James Johnson, and Thomas Mills, railway navigators, who were condemned at the Middlesex Sessions, on the 18th inst., to one month's imprisonment, with hard labour, for stealing a loaf, value 3½d., after they had suffered from starvation for two whole days ;" Charles Cochrane, Esq., in the chair—The chairman said he was greatly delighted to take the chair in furtherance of an object which was the most noble that could engross the attention of mankind— the promotion of mercy. They were called upon to defend some of their fellow-creatures who had fallen under the temptation of the circumstances in which they were placed to commit an offence which, under other circumstances they would not have been guilty of. They met to petition the Queen to pardon the men. He had no doubt that from one to two per day died on an average in London, of starvation, even as reported in the newspapers. He had exerted himself with the guardians of the poor, but all he

obtained was abuse ; but for that he did not care a rush. Last year they had a general fast, and this year thanksgivings for a good harvest ; but when the plenty came, had they relieved the distresses of the people consequent upon that abundance ? They had not. It was their duty when so much distress prevailed, to make sacrifices for the relief of the poor. For his own part, he had determined by March next, to give up the large house he now occupied, and to give up his carriage and horses, nor would he resume them until the poor were in better condition, and there were no more deaths from starvation. He then called upon Mr. Hoggins to propose the first resolution.—Mr. Hoggins, barrister-at-law, said, the State had a duty to feed her children, before it punished them for crimes which they committed through absolute want. This arose from a poor-law, which was cruel and unjust. It was known that an average poor rate, levied equally on all classes, of 1s. 7d. in the pound, would meet all that was now collected for the relief of the poor, whereas in many parishes, the poor man had to pay 10s. in the pound as his contribution to the poor rate. There was, however, no means of improving these evils, except by their united efforts. If all men were prepared to make the same sacrifices as their chairman, there would be no such distress as had been described that night. The Legislature had already done enough for the rich, they ought now to commence to do something for the poor. They should appoint a commission of inquiry into the wants of the people, to ascertain how they might be remedied.

Driven to Drink

Cheap gin brought oblivion to misery, but it created new misery of its own. It could be bought at all hours, even by children.

Illustrated London News.

There are few places in London where so great a variety of characters may be seen popping in and out in a short space of time, as at the bars of our modern gin-palaces. Even respectable men who meet each other by chance, after a long absence, must drop in at the nearest tavern, although thay have scarcely a minute to spare, to drink a glass together at the bar, and enquire about old friends. Married women, we are sorry to say, many of them the wives of clever mechanics, also congregate here, generally in the morning, when they go to market, and at a time when they ought to be providing the dinner for their families. Such things are thought but little of among those who are far from being numbered with the lowest orders of society. Then there are your itinerant vendors of almost every imaginable thing—these are, also, constant members of the bar, confining themselves generally to pennyworths of gin. The costermongers, who come wheeling and shouting from opposite directions, with their barrows, if they chance to meet near the door of a tavern, must, after a little gossip, go in and have their " drain."

Illustrated London News

Added to these, there are the poor, the old, and the miserable, who look and feel " half-dead," as they themselves express it, unless they are " lighted up " every two or three hours with a glass of spirits. Many of these have become so habituated to drink that they care but little for food, and very rarely partake of a substantial meal : a pennyworth of boiled shell-fish, such as whilks or mussels, an oyster or two, or a trotter, and sometimes a fried fish—all of which are borne into these places by hawkers every hour of the day—may be taken as fair samples of the food consumed by these regular drinkers.

Nor is it at the front of the gaudily fitted-up bars alone where such quantities of spirits are consumed. Women and children even are coming in with bottles ; some of the latter so little, that, like the one which our artist has so truthfully sketched, they are scarcely able to reach up and place the bottle upon the zinc-covered bar. If the weather is cold they are generally sent out in their mothers' shawls and bonnets, the one trailing upon the ground, and the other completely burying their little dirty faces. Even these young miserable creatures are fond of drink, and may sometimes be seen slily drawing the cork outside the door, and lifting the poisonous potion to their white withered lips. They have already found that gin numbs and destroys for a time the gnawing pangs of hunger, and they can drink the fiery mixture in its raw state.

Poverty and misery, and a want of the proper necessaries of life, have driven and are still driving hundreds to drink in this vast metropolis. Better food, better wages, and more employment are the only remedies that can be applied to this crying evil. They would sooner disperse a mob than all the police force with their staves.

Saved from a Life of Shame
Weekly Times, 13 August.

We have received a copy of an appeal for 6,000l., to complete the asylum for penitent females. Above one hundred and fifty degraded daughters of the poor, for the most part of a very tender age, pass through the adjoining hospital in the course of the year. The greater proportion of these having been faithfully instructed during their residence in the wards, express the most earnest desire to be saved from their life of shame. But whither can they go ? Exasperated relatives spurn them from their doors. Virtuous families refuse to employ or shelter them. What then remains for them, unless the helping hand of charity is stretched forth for their deliverance, but to revert to their former habits of infamy, in all human probability speedily to perish ? The committee are persuaded that when a humane public shall weigh the peculiar advantages possessed by this reformatory, in being able to select for its inmates those only of the patients of the hospital who have during their illness manifested the most satisfactory tokens of repentance, the requisite amount will be readily subscribed.

Competing to Enter an Orphanage
Illustrated London News, 17 June.

On Monday last an election of ten candidates took place in the Female Orphan Asylum, in which orphans are educated for domestic servants. Many of the distinguished and charitable of the nobility and gentry were present to conduct the polling of their respective *protégés*. The fact of there being only ten vacancies, and thirty-seven candidates, produced more than ordinary anxiety as to the result. One poor little unsuccessful orphan, whose twin and favourite sister is now in the asylum, was led away in extreme distress and heart-broken at her disappointment.

Unemployment Spreads

The depressed state of trade was responsible for much fresh unemployment, added to that of craftsmen like hand-loom weavers and the wool-combers of Bradford whose skills had been superseded by the ever-encroaching machines.

Weekly Times, 16 January.

A quotation, from the petition of the factory hands of Blackburn, will show the state of suffering in that town. It is dated November 12, 1847, and begins thus :—" Gentlemen, the weight of suffering cannot much longer be borne. We deprecate violence. We have no wish to touch the property of others, but we cannot submit to die of hunger. If the Celt could, the Saxon cannot. We see food around us in abundance ; but, without employment, that abundance is valueless unless the laws are faithfully administered (speaking of the Poor-laws)."

Scotland is no better off ; in Glasgow there are upwards of 2,500 unemployed and nearly all the mills running short time. At Kilbrachun, a Glasgow paper states, " That two-thirds of the working population are out of employment."

Throughout the country droves of railway labourers are roaming about, vainly supplicating for work, and subsisting on the givings of charity and the Poor-law Guardians. In South Staffordshire, the iron trade is in a woeful plight. The iron stone miners have received notice of a reduction of 20 per cent. in their wages ; short time is being generally introduced ; and many iron masters have determined upon suspending their works altogether. A short time before

the close of the last Session of Parliament, petitions were presented to the house of Commons, setting forth in melancholy terms the distress of the iron districts. Other statements from the provinces equally disheartening might be detailed ; but those already given are sufficient to show the state they are in. Let us now turn to London, the commercial emporium of the world, and examine its condition. Nothing can show this better than the annual report of the Mendicity Society, from which it appears that, in the twelve months ending in December, 1846, the number of persons relieved was 22,355 ; in the corresponding period of 1847, it was no less than 53,832. The number of meals provided by the society, in the former

Mansell

Lord Shaftesbury (in 1848, Ashley) was a Tory reformer responsible for making it illegal to employ women in mines, factory-workers for more than 10 hours a day, etc. Shaftesbury Avenue was named after him, and the statue of Eros in Piccadilly commemorates his love of mankind. Below : he visits a Ragged School (see page 61).

RTHPL

period, was 148,556 ; in the latter, 226,133 ; showing an increase in the number of persons relieved, for the year 1847, of 31,477 ; and in the number of meals provided, for the same year, of 77,877. These statistics show a fearful increase of poverty, so much so that the Mendicity Society is now calling on the public to recruit its almost exhausted funds. But there are many more evidences of poverty than this. At a meeting of the Spitalfields silk weavers, at Bethnal-green, on the 1st of last December, the following is a part of a resolution which was passed unanimously :—" The distress (of the weavers) being so fearfully extensive, the sufferings so unparalleled, and the loss of life so great, that they are such that the oldest inhabitant cannot remember having witnessed." Numbers of the poor and destitute of London, *lie on the cold and bare stones* of the streets, of the richest city on earth ; and the wind may blow, and the rain or snow may fall on the *shivering bodies* of these unfortunate wretches— while the rich man lies on his downy bed in a splendid mansion, and knows not or cares not for these destitute beings, *his fellow-creature's* flesh and blood, susceptible of pain like himself.

Go into any house, in any street in any town, and you will find every person complaining of the pressure of the times. Many are too proud to acknowledge their poverty. Others are living on a little money they may have saved, which they have withdrawn from the savings' bank, or building society. The withdrawals from these two useful institutions, during 1847, have greatly exceeded those of 1846. The middle class feel the effects of these *bad times* as well as others : for, if there be a great falling off in the earnings of the working classes, there is a great falling off in their spendings with the shop-keeper, whose custom decreases ; and thus his profits being smaller, he shares in the general depression which afflicts his poorer neighbour. Again, the failure of so many of our merchant princes, has not only ruined the prospects of their own families, but has turned adrift their servants, and brought to beggary, tradesmen dependent on the particular branch of trade which the capital of these merchants carried on.

Times like these suspend the progress of improvement among the people. All attention of working men is then directed to how they may live, not how they may improve their minds or morals. They are obliged to curtail their expenditure. The quantity and quality of their food is not so good. Their dwellings are not so well furnished. Themselves, their wives, and children are not so nicely clad. Their weekly newspaper or magazine is given up. Their children cease to go to school, and a sort of social disorganization takes place, like the present one we are suffering from ; and the serious aspect of which has never before been witnessed by the present generation, and I hope to God never will again. Such is the present condition of the working classes.

Wage Cuts

Britannia, 15 January.

We do not see without alarm and sorrow the general movement now taking place for reducing the wages of workmen in the manufacturing districts. Paragraphs like the following are becoming plentiful :—

" Blackburn.—Redution of Wages.— Friday week notices were posted in all the mills of the town apprizing the hands that *their wages would be reduced (generally 10 per cent.)* at the expiration of a month after date.—*Manchester Guardian.*

" Birmingham, Thursday.—The great quarterly meeting of ironmasters was held in the Town-hall today. In consequence of the present state of the trade, and the position assumed by the workmen, considerable importance was generally attached to the proceedings. Little business, however, was done, most of the works having suspended operations altogether, and the few that are employed working short time.

" Manchester, Jan. 11.—Without some change in the aspect of the market it is to be feared that the hours of labour must be again reduced. We hear from various quarters *that reductions of wages are quietly taking place, the workpeople seeing the utter inutility of struggling to resist them at a time when, even at the reduced rates proposed, their employers are losing money by everything they produce.*"

These reductions in wages are the inevitable effect of the poverty of the merchant and manufacturer. The operative will now have to balance his account between the new tariffs and a loss of ten per cent. on his wages. The degradation of his state has begun, but where will it end ? This deduction of two shillings in the pound is but the first instalment of the tribute he owes to free trade.

The Shop-Workers' Plight

Unlike the factory-workers, shop assistants had no protection against long hours, and many shops stayed open until midnight. In 1848 an Early Closing Association was formed to organize meetings and protest rallies.

Weekly Times, 30 January.

On Monday night, an aggregate meeting of the Assistant Drapers, Hosiers, Stationers, Hatters, &c., was held at the Commercial Rooms, Chelsea. The object of the meeting was to adopt a new scheme, inducing the public to lend their personal and pecuniary aid to carry out the desired design of the Association. There were three ways of putting an end to late hours ; first, by unanimity among the employers ; secondly, by an Act of Parliament ; and thirdly, by the influence of the public. The British public would respond to their appeal, when shown that the late hours tend to crush health and every noble aspiration. It would be ere long evident to all that the public would find a very great advantage by purchasing by day than by night ; for it frequently happens the drapers and others boast of making a greater profit from the public through late dealing. Mr. A. Leggatt proposed a resolution to the following effect :—" That late hours business is an evil of very great magnitude, not only to assistants but to society."

England's White Slaves

This is what the dressmakers were called. With sewing-machines and ready-made clothes a thing of the future, in London

alone 15,000 women worked at this trade. But the vogue for French fashions (even favoured by the Queen) made it hard for them to get work. This is an extract from a petition they sent to Lord Ashley (Shaftesbury).

Weekly Times, 2 July, and British Banner, 20 September.

During eight or nine months in the year hundreds of those who are termed out-door-workers are in the habit of walking daily from one house of business to another for employment, and are generally informed that they are incapable, and that none but French women are engaged ; and when in the busy season we do obtain work, 6s. per week and our tea are the usual wages. And as to food, that many of us are strangers to any regular meal, and have been long suffering silently the severest privations, is a notorious fact.

We would earnestly recommend the dressmakers to form a *society among themselves*, and not to work for any employer who refuses to reduce the hours of labour from twelve and fifteen (what they are at present) to nine or at the most ten hours a day. This much desired reform, besides greatly conducing to our health, would be the means of giving increased employment ; for as it is now, we labour almost incessantly by day, and often deep

Illustrated London News, 26 August.

Some of the Paris fashions which were putting the English dressmakers out of work in London.

into the hours of midnight, and thus obviously diminish the demand for out-door labour, as in a hurried order for the Court mourning or a drawing-room, one person does the work of three. Very many of us would gladly emigrate (if assisted by Government), to gain that subsistence in another country which we vainly endeavour to obtain in our own. The time has, we think, come when the Legislature might interfere for our protection, and pass some ten-hour bill for us : so that after a life of slavery and toil—when our weary hands are no longer able to draw the needle—we may not have before us the dreary prospect of the hospital or the workhouse.

The shirt-makers of London pay fifteen pence for making a dozen shirts, and a female thus employed could not earn more than 3¾d per day !

Bakers also roasted the dinners of the artisans for them : home-bakery was already a lost art in the cities.

Illustrated London News (a drawing by Leech), 25 December.

Song of the Loaf

Another of the many trades where intolerable conditions and long hours (18-20) were still endured for low wages (16 shillings to 27 shillings a week) was bakery.

In a stifling room and small,
    I saw, by an oven door.
A man who seem'd ready to faint and fall
    On the flags of the heated floor :
His cheeks they were wan and pale ;
    His eyes they were sunk and dim ;
And it seem'd as if Nature ere long would fail,
    And earth be no more for him.

It was work, work, work,
    Till his pulse grew weak and low ;
It was work, work, work,
    Till his limbs could scarcely go.
No time had his body to gain
    Delight from the summer skies ;
No spirit or strength had his mind to obtain
    The knowledge that makes men wise.

Hanging : a Public Spectacle

Weekly Times, 16 January.

On Monday morning, at eight o'clock, this wretched man [*Thomas Sale*] underwent the extreme penalty of the law in front of Newgate, for the murder and highway robbery of Mr. Bellchambers, in Westminster.

Long before the hour of six o'clock, although the morning was dark and piercingly cold, a number of persons had collected in the vicinity, consisting principally of young boys, lads, costermongers, and girls of the lowest description. The sheriffs arrived at the prison shortly before seven, and after this time the crowd began to pour in from all parts in shoals, and by eight o'clock every avenue in the vicinity of the gaol where a sight could be obtained was densely crowded. Precisely as the clock of St. Sepulchre's struck eight, the bell commenced tolling, and in less than two minutes the Rev. Mr. Davis ascended the scaffold, reading the burial service, followed by Sale, who walked firmly up the steps. He looked boldly at the crowd, and having made a low bow without uttering a word, took his station under the fatal beam. The executioner immediately placed the cap over his head, and in another minute he was launched into eternity.

The behaviour of the crowd on this occasion was, for the most part, decorous—at least until the execution was actually over ; although the anxiety to gain a view of the scaffold caused a good deal of pushing and some little fighting, there was no intentional violation of the principles of decency. At the same time there seemed to be no feeling of the solemnity and awful nature of the proceedings going on, which appeared to be chiefly regarded as a passing means of temporary excitement. All feeling of solemnity was greatly militated against by the fact that those in the part of the crowd not immediately surrounding the scaffold being generally unable to see over the heads of those in front of them, kept jumping off the ground incessantly to catch a glimpse at the scene on the gallows. The incessant jumping gave the crowd an appearance like that of a tribe of savages dancing a death dance, and utterly

A crowd gathers to watch a hanging outside Newgate. Illustrated London News.

prevented those who were engaged in it from feeling any thing of the impressiveness which should attach to exhibition of the kind. Arrangements existed in the crowd in the shape of stools, chairs, fruit barrows, &c., for enabling those who chose to pay a few pence for the accommodation to see over the heads of the crowd. Sundry fights took place between the owners of these chairs and barrows and persons who endeavoured to spring upon them unobserved for the sake of evading the fee, and the general manner of the crowd differed little from what is observable at reviews and other out-of door gratuitous spectacles. The members of the crowd were for the most part of the lowest class : costermongers, prostitutes, and pickpockets evidently formed the chief part, but there were also many mechanics and persons who appeared to belong to the class of tradesmen. At the windows around also appeared many persons who were at all events dressed like gentlemen, and even well-dressed women were lookers on therefrom the whole time. The greater number of the persons present remained on the spot long after the man was dead, and during the interval between the actual hanging and the cutting down, which seemed to be the two parts of the process which excited the most interest. The gallows seemed to be looked upon with the most perfect indifference and laughter, and coarse jokes were rife among the mob. A few minutes before nine some slight excitement began to revive, and the barrow men again called to the crowd " to pay a penny to see the man cut down," and then some comic incident occurring, shouts of laughter were allowed free vent, and so with talking, and fighting, and laughing, the hour during which the body was suspended passed away. When the executioner appeared upon the scaffold again, the death dance was recommended. Men held their children on their shoulders to " see the sight ;" and although, as the body was cut down and borne away, a slight shudder seemed to take place among a few persons, the majority were as unaffected as before. Immediately afterwards the crowd began to disperse, many of the men evidently determined to make a holiday of it.

Undeserving Poor

The pitiless morality of the times withheld any charity from those who transgressed. (Mr. Carker rides by the starving prostitute whose ruin he had caused.)
Dickens' Dombey & Son, *Cruikshank drawing.*

Jarndyce Books

RAILWAY MANIA

Though thousands of miles of new lines were still being laid, the golden age of rail was drawing to a close. A proliferation of uneconomic lines was leading to big losses. There were now mounting criticisms of the discomforts and dangers of some trains, and of the inconveniences arising from the differing widths of track favoured by various companies. On the other hand, the vast social changes brought by the railways were now being appreciated. Speed of transport meant farmers and fishers could supply inland towns with fresh produce. It brought a revolution to the newspapers and the mails. For the first time, it was possible (and necessary) to iron out the big discrepancies in time recorded on the nation's clocks. And the railways guaranteed the employment of hundreds of thousands of men—in their own service, in the coal and iron industries, and in the timber trade. They also had an effect on housing ; commuting was now possible, and so the suburban sprawl began.

Illustrated London News.

George Stephenson died in 1848. As a boy he worked in the mines, and later invented a safety-lamp (in the same year as Humphry Davy's). He designed the first viable steam locomotive (in 1814) and thus started the railway revolution.

Too Many Lines

The railway-building spree of previous years slowed up a bit as it was realized that too many uneconomic lines were being laid.

Economist, 21 October.

Capital has already been subscribed and paid up, or borrowed, for railways completed and in the course of construction in the United Kingdom, in round figures to the extent of *two hundred millions.* The best shares are not now worth half their value at that time. The *two hundred millions* of capital already expended, has been chiefly used in constructing great trunk lines in the most favourable situations, and many of them, taken by themselves, would no doubt continue to pay large profits. The *one hundred and thirty millions* yet to be expended applies to lines in the least favourable positions, and to small branch lines, which, all recent experience has shown, will pay little or no profit, but in respect to which the great trunk lines are compromised, either in the form of guarantees or as actual properties, and the real effect of which must be to charge upon them whatever losses are sustained by these inferior lines. This fact lies at the bottom of all the existing railway difficulties, and the utter want of confidence on the part of capitalists.

Too Many Trains

Illustrated London News

The fall of stock has spoken in language so plain of impending ruin, unless a change of system be adopted—that attempts have been made to save expense by effecting amalgamations of the great lines ; and schemes have been debated whereby the fares would be raised to the public, and a morning and evening train substituted for the hourly or even half-hourly trains that now whirl us from one end of the country to the other. There can be no doubt, we think, that union for the purposes of cheap and efficient management would answer its object. But already some, if not all, of these companies, have shown themselves tyrannical enough. To compel people to travel in first-class carriages, they have made second-class carriages as uncomfortable as they dared ; and had it not been for the forcible interference of the State, their carriages for the poor would have been little if any better than the trucks for the conveyance of cattle.

In France and Belgium, where the State has exercised a more careful supervision over Railway management, the carriages for second-class passengers are as comfortable as first-class carriages with us ; and the mercenary tyranny of rendering poverty unnecessarily uncomfortable has not been resorted to. This is but one of many forms of public evil, which these great monopolies may assume.

The telegraph (see page 77) brought news of the Paris revolution at unprecedented speed to a public avid for information.

Lady's Newspaper, 26 August.

MAC—BULL AND THE RAILWAY WITCHES.

*John Bull wonders what the railway
powers will inflict on him next.*

Punch

A Question of Gauge

Vituperative debate now raged over the question of gauges (width of railway tracks). The Great Western had been built to a 7-foot gauge unusable by trains built to run on 4 ft 8½ in- tracks, the European standard. (The narrow-gaugers eventually won, and the G.W.R. had to lay new tracks.)

Pamphlet : " An Appeal on behalf of the Farmers and Miners of Devon and Cornwall, against the last decision of an Ex-Commissioner of Railways. "

There can be no doubt that if the national system of railways, which runs in an unbroken chain from Gloucester to Birmingham, Derby, and the northern coal-fields, to the ports of London, Hull, and Liverpool, had been extended to Bristol and Exeter, Plymouth and Falmouth, those richly agricultural districts would have, on the one hand, derived great advantage from new markets for their agricultural and mining produce ; and on the other, for the manufactured articles sent either for exchange or export.

The projectors of the western lines chose to adopt a wide exceptional gauge, unlike anything that has ever been adopted in any other country in the world ; the effect of which has been to destroy the harmony of the British railway system, by preventing what it is the great object of a perfect railway system to effect—a continuous conveyance of merchandise.

The whole plan of the broad gauge was based upon a common, but utterly mistaken, theory. Mr. Brunel thought that a very few great main lines only would be made, and that a very few daily trains of great size, for either goods or passengers, would be required. He therefore prepared a vast machine of great capacity, something like the unfortunate " Great Britain " steamer, which must have rendered her owners bankrupt if she had not run ashore, as she was of so large a tonnage that she could never have obtained a reasonably full cargo within a reasonable time.

Instead of this big train and truck theory, the more railway traffic became developed, the more necessary it became to send frequent trains, and to send for merchandise trains single trucks from every roadside station, whether loaded or half loaded. The result was, and is, that on all railways many trains per day go half loaded and a half-loaded broad gauge carriage or truck is a much more serious thing than either of narrow-gauge dimensions—it is nearly double the weight. Mr. Brunel met the difficulties of a break of gauge in his usual audacious style. Having denied that such a thing could occur, he now denied that, having occurred, it was any difficulty at all. He promised to lift iron, coals, eggs, watches, pigs, bulls, crockery, and glass from one gauge to the other, at no expense of time or money. Of course, if the public had thought there were to have been difficulties of this kind, Mr. Brunel could never have carried out his crotchet.

I. K. Brunel was the great engineer of the railways, and of the huge new steamship of the era.

Death on the Rails

Rail accidents were as commonplace as road accidents today.

Illustrated London News, 13 May.

On Wednesday an accident occurred to the Express train from Exeter, which resulted in the death of six persons, and the serious injury of several others. The train consisted of two first and four second-class carriages, which were drawn by an engine (the Sultan) and tender. Its progress was uninterrupted till it approached the Shrivenham station, where it is stated that the signal was given that the line was clear. At the angle of divergence of the off-line was an empty horse-box with a truck attached (on which was a gentleman's carriage), which it is supposed just overlapped the main up line, as a collision took place. The second-class carriage was dashed to pieces. The unfortunate passengers were flung out in every direction. The line was strewd with the wreck of the carriage, while a number of the passengers, wounded and dying, were lying about. It is unnecessary to add that the greatest alarm prevailed among the passengers in the other carriages.

Great Train Robbery

Security was as limited as safety, and reports like these regularly appeared in the press.

Illustrated London News, 15 January.

Another extensive robbery has been committed, under circumstances of a peculiarly mysterious nature, from the Great Western Railway Company. A box of sovereigns—it is said amounting to several thousand pounds—was deposited in one of the carriages, and was, up to the time of the starting of the train from London, seen properly safe. On the arrival of the carriages at Bristol, it was found that the golden treasure had been abstracted. The box had been perforated by means of a circular saw or some cutting instrument of the kind. It is said that six persons, having the appearance of gentlemen, engaged the box of the railway carriage next to that in which the gold was deposited, and some suspicion has fallen on them, it being supposed that they belong to the London swell mob.

Attempt to Destroy a Passenger Train.—At the quarter sessions held at Cardiff, William Scott was sentenced to seven years' transportation, for wilfully and maliciously attempting to overturn a passenger train on the Taff Vale Railway, by removing the rails.

How They Brought the Good News

The coming of the railways revolutionized some old trades, and created new ones. For the first time, the cities could be brought fresh milk and fish from the farms and ports. And news hot from the presses. The vast W. H. Smith chain owed its beginnings to the railways that supplied its station stalls (new in 1848) with papers.

Illustrated London News, 26 February.

One of the most extraordinary achievements in newspaper expressing was performed on Saturday last. A special express, which was arranged by Messrs. W. H. Smith and Son, newsvendors, Strand, left London at 35 minutes past five o'clock in the morning, with the newspapers of the day, and reached Glasgow at fifty-seven minutes past three in the afternoon, completing the journey of 472½ miles in ten hours and twenty-two minutes. The detentions amounted to fifty minutes, including eight minutes occupied in passing from Gateshead to the Newcastle station, and seven minutes in passing from Tweedmouth to the station at Berwick, thus reducing the actual railway travelling to nine hours and thirty-two minutes, being at the rate of fifty miles an hour !

The Electric Telegraph

Still a novelty, the telegraph was first used by the railway companies for controlling their traffic, and soon was adopted by the Press too.

Railway and Commercial Journal, 23 December.

The Electric Telegraph Company have

established a continuous line of communication between London and Edinburgh. This will affect, it is said, a saving of one to two hours in the transmission of intelligence.

The Cambrian engine, new in 1848. "... splendid new locomotive ... novel an[d] pleasing appearance ... a beautif[ul] mechanical movement."
Mechanics Magazine, 3 June.

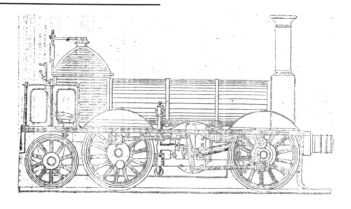

COOK'S
SCOTTISH TOURIST
PRACTICAL
DIRECTORY:
A GUIDE
TO THE

Principal Tourist Routes, Conveyances,

AND

SPECIAL TICKET ARRANGEMENTS,

SANCTIONED BY

RAILWAY, STEAMBOAT AND COACH COMPANIES,

COMMANDING THE HIGHLAND EXCURSION TRAFFIC.

BY THOMAS COOK,

Tourist Manager, London and Leicester.

WITH A

SERIES OF NEW SECTIONAL MAPS,

Drawn and Engraved specially for the work by
W. & A. K. JOHNSTON, Edinburgh.

LONDON:
THOS. COOK, TOURIST OFFICE, 98, FLEET-STREET;
AND ALL BOOKSELLERS.

Another fortune created by the railwa[y] system, for Mr. Cook and his tours. A Baptist travelling missionary, the firs[t] excursion he ran was to a temperanc[e] conference in Loughborough in 1841.

A Navvie's Life

The railways were built by navigator[s] (navvies): rough, often drunken, violent—living a life apart from the rest of th[e] community. Their work was dangerous a[s] well as hard, particularly when buildin[g] tunnels, and they were sometimes cheate[d] of their pay.

Northern Star (reader's letter), 5 February

Sir,—My attention has been attracted t[o] the different means that have bee[n] proposed for the better defence of th[e] nation, and amongst these I find there ar[e] parties who recommend the enrolment o[f] the railway labourers (for that purpose) who are now out of employment. I woul[d] ask what have the railway labourers t[o] defend? I have worked on differen[t] railways, and have never seen anythin[g] worth the defending except it be slavery tommy shops, fever sheds, and many thing[s] more, that are repugnant to the laws o[f] equity and humanity. I ask, is slave[r]y worth defending, where the poor man i[s] driven to work like a beast, and in man[y] cases compelled to work in places where his life is in imminent danger every moment, to satisfy the avarice of a greedy contractor ? Is the truck system worth defending—a system both unjust and cruel ? Instead of the workman getting his wages every week, and spending it to the best advantage, he is compelled to take inferior goods out of the tommy shop, and pay the highest price for them, and, in most instances, short weight in the bargain. And I have actually known the pay day put off for nine weeks, in order to compel the men to take their goods from the shop ; and any man that was discontent was sent to the office for his money, and had no more employment. There are also what we term the fever sheds, which the masters build, by nailing a few half-inch boards together. Their dimensions are, generally, six yards by five on the ground floor, and many of them without any other apartments ; and I have known twenty human beings—men women and children— pig together in these miserable huts, for which the tenant has paid *six shillings per week*. So much for your humane railway contractors. These are the noble institutions they wish us to defend. But the navvies are not such idiots as all that. Although they are generally termed an ignorant and immoral class of men, yet they are a class that are beginning to boldly assert their rights as men, and as citizens of the world. Though we are ignorant our motto is, " No vote, no musket."

A " navvie ", Berwick-on-Tweed.

Railway Navvies' Song

In eighteen hundred and forty-one
Me corderoy breeches I put on
   to work upon the railway,
The railway, I'm weary of the railway.
Poor Paddy works on the railway.

In eighteen hundred forty-two,
From high pitch school I moved a crew
And found myself a job to do
A-working on the railway.

I was wearing corderoy breeches,
   digging ditches, pulling switches,
   counting hitches,
I was working on the railway.

In eighteen hundred forty-three,
I packed me shovel across me knee
And went to work for the company
On the Leeds and Selby Railway.

In eighteen-hundred and forty-eight,
I learned to take my whisky straight,
'Tis an illygant drink and can't be bate,
For working on the railway.

I was wearing corderoy breeches,
   digging ditches, pulling switches,
   counting hitches,
I was working on the railway.

Building the railway approaches to Waterloo Bridge, July 1848.

RTHPL

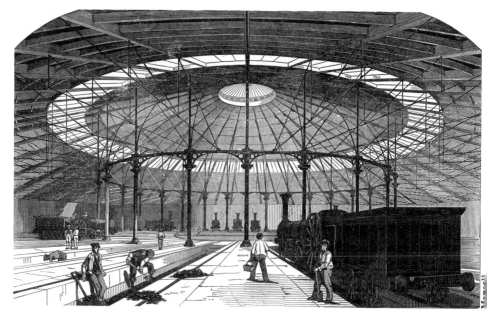

Pride in the new railways was expressed in their architecture, and in new engineering feats. Below: Accrington Viaduct.

Above : The Round House, at Camden Town (used for turning engines). Railway-building at Camden Town featured in Dombey & Son, *published in 1848.*

Illustrated London News

THE GREAT CLOCK MOVEMENT.

Greenwich Clock, loq. "COME, NO STOPPING—YOU MUST MOVE ON."

Greenwich Time tells the disputatious clocks of Britain to keep in step. (Only the speed of rail travel now enabled big discrepancies in time shown on the clocks of different cities to be adjusted.)

Punch.

SEDITION IN IRELAND

Years of poverty and a succession of potato famines had reduced Ireland to misery. Many tenants unable to pay rent were ruthlessly evicted by landlords (often living in England). Those who could raise the fare emigrated, mostly to America. At a time when anti-Catholicism was very much alive even in England, religious strife added fuel to the smouldering fires of revolt. But revolt would inevitably fail : in the words of a letter from Carlyle, " Ireland is like a half-starved rat that crosses the path of an elephant. What must the elephant do ? Squelch it—by heavens—squelch it. "

Strong Hand of the Law

A special commission was set up to try the mounting number of " turbulent and disaffected " lawbreakers. In England there was little understanding of the conditions that helped to produce them. Sentences were harsh.

Lady's Newspaper, 15 January.

Three of the prisoners have been convicted of murder and left for execution, whilst a number of others have been sentenced to transportation and imprisonment, in some extending over the whole term of their lives. The culprits in every instance belonged to the labouring classes, and most of them, as they appeared at the bar before the Lord Chief Justice, wore the calm, yet scowling, air of desperate men.

Every one must regret, of course, the necessity of the extraordinary means adopted to ensure that security of life and property in Ireland ; but, whilst the idle and reckless habits so characteristic of the lower orders of its inhabitants excite them to deeds of violence on the first excuse of famine or of oppression, it is only common justice to apply the strong hand of the law for the protection of the peaceable and honest among them, who have laudably provided for the exigencies of life, to which all are equally exposed.

Preaching Rebellion

The first issue of Mitchel's newspaper was incitement to throw off English rule.

United Irishman, 12 February.

The only hope of the liberation of this country lies in a movement in which all classes and creeds of Irishmen shall be fairly represented and by which the interests of none shall be endangered.

Inasmuch as English legislation threatens all Irishmen with a common ruin, we entertain a confident hope their common necessities will speedily unite Irishmen in an effort to get rid of it.

A peasant's cabin.
Lady's Newspaper

A mother begs for her starving family.

The Influence of the Priesthood

Incitement to violence was also supplied by the church. (Later, the British government prevailed on the Pope to curb these activities of the priests in Ireland.)

Banner of Britain, 14 January.
(quoting Prussian State Gazette).

It is impossible for any one who is acquainted with the condition of the people of Ireland, their absolute dependence on the priesthood, the access of the Popish priest to the conscience of each individual by means of the confessional, and the whole tendency of this infernal war,—it is impossible, we say, for such a one to doubt that the priests are informed of each individual assassination. The Romish Church, with its agitating and absolving priests, is therefore in Ireland the great confederate in crimes, which, in their cruelty and bloodthirstiness, are not exceeded by the accumulated horrors of the night of St. Bartholomew in France. Let the public imagine what the moral condition of such a people must be when their very religion is blood-stained.

No Repeal of the Union

Agitation to dissolve the union of Ireland with England came to nothing. The " repealers " themselves were divided, with Old Ireland led by O'Connell and Young Ireland by O'Brien (M.P. for Limerick) and Mitchel—the latter pressing for action by arms, O'Connell believing in negotiation and petitions.

Times, 31 March.

Here is the " appeal " which is to be presented by a deputation to the Queen :—
" May it please your Majesty—
" We inhabit an island, capable from its fertility, its harbours, its fisheries, and its mineral and other great natural resources, of rivaling the most prosperous countries on the face of the globe.
" The inhabitants of this island have for centuries furnished soldiers for the armies and sailors for the fleets of England, and have thus aided to place it on the lofty pinnacle whereon it now stands among the nations of the earth.
" Before the union of Great Britain with Ireland we, your Irish subjects, were a happy, prosperous, and thriving people.

" Since that union we have become a miserable, poverty-stricken, famished population.

" To that union we can trace, in unmistakeable characters, all our misery and unutterable woe.

" To repeal that union we have in vain appealed to the Imperial Legislature.

" As our last constitutional resource we now approach your Most Gracious Majesty."

The British Forces Move In

Times, 3 and 6 April ; Britannia, 29 July

Paris, after the entrance of the allied armies in 1815, could scarcely have presented a more belligerent appearance than the Irish metropolis does on the 4th of April, 1848. The streets swarm with red coats, varied by the blue uniforms of the Artillery and light cavalry. Barracks, temporary it is to be hoped, are rearing their fronts in quarters hitherto devoted to the peaceful purposes of science and commerce.

Orders have been issued by the Admiralty to the war-steamers at the various dockyards to get their steam up and bank their fires so as to be ready to start at a moment's notice. The Llewellyn steam-vessel left Woolwich yesterday with three waggon-loads of rockets for Ireland.

The remainder of the 57th Regiment disembarked at the North-wall this morning, and marched into barracks. On landing at the quay the soldiers were loudly hissed and hooted by the mob.

Nowise daunted by the preparations of Government, the cry of " Arm, arm," raised by Mr. Mitchell, is being cheerfully responded to by the mob of Dublin. The run for pikes is rather on the increase, and to meet the demand very inferior weapons are vended in Patrick-street.

The 'Gagging Act'

The government sought to suppress seditious publications such as The United Irishman *by the Crown and Government Security Act.*

Times (quoting The Freeman*), 12 April.*

The Whig Ministry have propounded their remedy for the deep discontent that now festers in the hearts of Irishmen.

That remedy is the transport ship.

Wearied with our importunity, the British Minister, instead of yielding our just demands, insolently commands us to be silent, and brings in a bill to award the brand of felon and perpetual exile to every Irishman who hereafter may " express, utter, or declare, by publishing and printing, or writing, or by open or advised speaking," his resolve that Ireland shall be again a nation.

Mitchel Transported

Among others brought to trial was Mitchel, sentenced to transportation. Public sympathy for him led to demonstrations and protests.

Dublin Evening Mail, 24 May ; Times, 30 May ; and Irish Felon, 24 June.

A notice has been distributed and placarded throughout Dublin, Kildare, and Meath, and other counties, on behalf of Mr. Mitchell, to the following effect :—

" Hear ye now or never, men of Ireland. The cause of tenant-farmers and of our country is to be tried in the person of John Mitchell. March ye, therefore, to Dublin—you whose life or death hangs on his trial.

" Your enemies are packing a jury to assassinate him. March and see that he gets a fair trial, or if he be foully condemned avenge him and save yourselves. Show this to all your neighbours, and give it all publicity."

The transportation of a man, as a felon, for uttering sentiments held and professed by at least five-sixths of his countrymen, seemed to me so violent and so insulting a national wrong, that submission to it must be taken to signify incurable slavishness. The English government, the proclaimed enemy of our nationality, had deliberately selected John Mitchel to wreak their vengeance upon him, as representative of the Irish nation. By indicting him for " felony " they virtually indicted five-sixths of the Irish people for " felony.' By sentencing him to fourteen years' transportation to a penal settlement, they pronounced five-sixths of the Irish people guilty of a crime worthy of such punishment. They occupy our country with military force, in our despite, making barracks of our very marts and colleges. They pervert our police force into an organisation of street bullies, as if to drive all peace-loving industrious citizens into the ranks of disaffection. They insult the poor dupes of " legal and constitutional " agitation, and rudely open their eyes to the real nature of foreign rule by such an outrage upon public decency and justice as this " trial."

Call to Arms

Repressive measures were counter-productive. Hundreds of clubs rapidly formed with the aim of driving the British out.

Irish Times, 24 June.

We offer these " fundamental rules,' which we unhesitatingly recommend to free this country from the curse of British rule.

1. That no youth under sixteen years of age be eligible to become a member.

2. That no man be permitted to continue a member who is not armed within a fortnight after his admission.

3. That no member shall be considered armed who, furnished with a rifle or musket, is not provided with, at least, one hundred rounds of ball cartridges ; or, possessed of a pike-head, has not a ten-foot ash pole attached to it.

4. That each member subscribe at least one penny a week to enable their brother members possessed of a musket or rifle, in the city clubs to practise daily, if possible, in the shooting galleries ; and, in the country ones, to provide themselves with powder and ball for a like purpose—it being provided in the latter case that an effigy of Clarendon [*Governor-General of Ireland*], placed upon the mound most conveniently remote from the ears of a policeman, do act as bull's-eye.

Clarendon Acts

Times, 20 July

Proclamations will be issued this evening, declaring the city and county of Dublin,

the city of Cork and three baronies in the county, the city of Waterford and three baronies in the county, and the town of Drogheda, to be in a state of disturbance ; the effect of which will be that all persons not duly qualified must deliver up their arms within nine days from the date of the proclamation.

Disraeli Speaks

Fears of the revolutionary movement in Europe lay behind the government's swift repression of Irish rebels.

Times, 24 July

Mr. Disraeli declared his intention of giving the measure of Government his unvarying and unequivocal support. If he could bring himself to think that this pending insurrection arose from the social and political grievances of Ireland, and that this bill would be an obstacle to the remedy of those grievances [*suspending Habeas Corpus*], he should be inclined to view it with distrust. Its character was flagrant ; it was avowedly an invasion of the constitution. He considered this pending insurrection to be neither an agrarian nor a religious movement. It was nothing more or less than a Jacobin movement. Now, looking as he did, upon Jacobinism as a system of unmitigated fraud and violence, we must encounter its violence with greater force.

Benjamin Disraeli.

Habeus Corpus Suspended

Within three days, Parliament rushed legislation through to enable agitators to be held without trial. Rebel newspapers were suppressed.

Times, 24 July and
Lady's Newspaper, 30 July.

The announcement of Lord John Russell's intentions to apply this day to Parliament for additional powers to crush insurrection reached here [*Ireland*] by electric telegraph early in the forenoon, and had a thunderbolt fallen upon the city it could not have created greater dismay or terror. Full time was it to resort to the extreme measure shadowed forth in the Premier's notice of motion, and that not another instant is to be lost will be made tolerably clear by a perusal of the manifestoes—it would be childishness to call them newspaper articles—put forward in the felon journal of this day's date. They are " open and advised " declarations of war, and nothing less. Those blood-breathing documents tell the people that the hour has come for striking the blow ; that the 40,000 military composing the Irish garrison must be slaughtered ; that they (the people) are to be stigmatized as cowards for evermore should they neglect the present opportunity to obliterate British dominion in Ireland. All this, and even more desperate advice, is given by the accredited leaders of the movement, so that there is no choice left ; the crisis cannot be much longer averted.

The only attempt at a rising fizzled out within three days. Its sole " battle " was a skirmish around Widow McCormack's cottage. A few days later, O'Brien was arrested, and all revolt was over.

Illustrated London News

Smith O'Brien in the dock. He was sentenced to be hanged, drawn and quartered after being tried by a jury from which Catholics were excluded. He was later reprieved.

Lady's Newspaper, 14 October.

The Potato Crop Fails

The terrible potato famine of 1845 was still fresh in people's minds when blight struck again. Once more, starvation threatened.

Times, 25 and 31 July and 10 August.

Misfortunes, it is said, seldom come single. The weather continues wet, cold, and harsh, and, without giving heed to all the croakings of the ravens, it is unfortunately undeniable that the accounts of the potato blight are becoming daily more numerous. The idea of another famine, super-added to the probabilities of an insurrection, is too fearful for contemplation.

We regret that it is our duty to state, that it is probable that this unfortunate country will this year also suffer a considerable loss of that crop which, despite the warnings of the past seasons of suffering, is still, in many parts of Ireland, the chief dependence of the farmer. Our readers are aware that we have diligently laboured to convince the farmer that it was madness to rely upon a single uncertain plant for food, and that sound husbandry required that other crops should be substituted for a portion of the potatoes which in former years he was accustomed to grow. Unfortunately, the idea that the disease would not again attack the crop somehow or other got possession of the public mind and induced our farmers to recommend its extended cultivation.

Winter Evictions

Dispirited, hungry and penniless, the Irish now had another prospect of famine and evictions to face. From every district reports of their distresses multiplied.

Illustrated London News, 24 June ;
Bradford Observer, 7 December ; and
Tipperary Vindicator, December.

A larger number of persons have been this year ejected than within any similar period within the oldest remembrance. Almost daily the sheriff, or his deputy, is engaged in the sad and melancholy work of levelling the houses of the rural population, who have no resource except the workhouse— not even the workhouse in many unions now, as, with few exceptions, all those institutions are densely crowded.

Evictions seem to multiply as the winter advances ; 66 human beings were lately turned out of their holdings in the Skibbereen union, and in the neighbourhood of Carrick-on-Suir 16 families, consisting of 80 individuals were ejected, for non-payment of rent, and 8 houses levelled. Murders and outrages are again becoming common. In Roscommon the villages swarm with soldiers, engaged in collecting poor rates ; for, says a local

After forcibly evicting tenants, their cottages were destroyed.

Illustrated London News, 16 December.

correspondent, " without the sabre and the bayonet no money will be paid !"

Whole districts are cleared. Not a roof-tree is to be seen where the happy cottage of the labourer at no distant day cheered the landscape. The ditch side, the dripping rain, and the cold sleet are the covering of the wretched outcast the moment the cabin is tumbled over him ; for who has the temerity to afford him hospitality, when the warrant has been signed for his extinction ? There are vast tracts of the most fertile land in the world now thrown out of tillage. There are no symptoms of life within their borders, no more than if they were situated in the midst of the Great Desert.

Encampment in Phoenix Park, Dublin. *Illustrated London News.*

Forging pikes for the Irish rebels.

RTHPL

GETTING AWAY FROM IT ALL

The desperation of life at home helped to build an Empire abroad. Despite the long voyages (steam was only just beginning to replace sail) and sometimes appalling conditions packed in the holds, artisans and others saved every penny to emigrate. Government and public opinion gave them every encouragement to go.

A Tide of Overpopulation

Emigration was seen as the answer to city over-population and its consequences : unemployment, poverty and crime.

British Banner, 20 September.

There are, in the Metropolis, at this moment, 200,000 workmen, of whom one-third are in full employment, one-third partially employed,—pawning their clothes and furniture for a miserable subsistence, and supplying the deficiency by the scant boons of casual charity,—and the remaining third are wholly without occupation, and dependent upon others for a wretched pittance to keep soul and body together. There are multitudes of industrious, religious, and every way superior men, who would gladly emigrate, but who are prevented by the lack of means. They are already so impoverished, in many cases so embarrassed, and so near the very gate of the workhouse—that should they pine and die at home, they cannot transport themselves to the Colonies. But to the colonies, by some means, they must be conveyed, or no man can foresee the afflictions into which the nation will be plunged by the ever-rising tide of over population.

"Worthy Objects" to Send to the Colonies

Government, charities, self-help groups and even trades unions did all they could to finance emigrants. By such means, ¼ million people left during the year for America, Canada and Australia.

Family Herald, Weekly Times, 17 September.

The government contemplates an immediate application to parliament, for authority to raise a loan for emigration. The amount will be at least £500,000, perhaps £1,000,000.

The committee of the Philanthropic Society have reported that they hope to have a model farm opened. In this establishment criminal and vagrant boys will be taught gardening, field-labour, and all pursuits proper to be known to agricultural emigrants.

A numerous public meeting for the purpose of receiving the report of a committee appointed to inquire into the practicability of forming an emigration club for the working classes. The report proposed that the subscribers should pay 9d. per week per share, and that the election of members for emigration should take place every three months, and be decided by a lot.

On Wednesday the "Duchess of Northumberland" left with a considerable number of emigrants on board, for Australia. Amongst them were four young men who had been received into the Ragged-school, Marylebone, who, being selected as worthy objects, were, with their wives and children (amounting altogether to eleven individuals), at the expense of the committee, both for passage and outfit, sent out to Port Philip, as labourers. The committee will send out two more men next week.

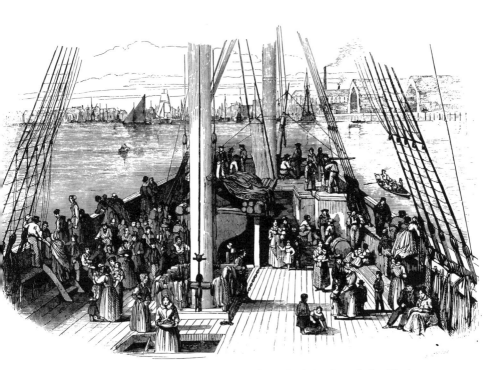

The " Artemisia " was a highly praised ship in which emigrants went out under the supervision of a doctor, and were placed in work by government agents when they arrived in Australia. Food and hygiene were good. Before departure, the Prayer-book and Homily Society distributed their wares to the passengers.

Illustrated London News, 12 August.

Five Months Under Sail

To emigrate (particularly to Australia) called for considerable fortitude, yet tens of thousands went.

British Banner, May.

A voyage of four or five months [to Australia], is fraught with an alarm which quickly represses every rising emotion in behalf of emigration. If that fine country could be reached, on an average, in the space of a month, or six weeks, we believe that thousands would be inclined to proceed thither. There is but one way to overcome this serious obstacle to the prosperity of the colony and the consequent relief of Great Britain,—the application of steam.

The Dispirited and the Dying

On some ships, particularly from Ireland to America or Canada, emigrants were ruthlessly exploited ; and many never survived the voyage. This is one emigrant's account of conditions (quoted by W. A. Carruthers in Emigration from the British Isles).

Before the emigrant has been a week at sea he is an altered man. How can it be otherwise ? Hundreds of poor people, men, women and children of all ages, from the drivelling idiot of ninety to the babe just born, huddled together without light, without air, wallowing in filth and breathing a fetid atmosphere, sick in body, dispirited in heart, the fever patients lying between the sound ; living without food or medicine, except as administered by the hand of casual charity, dying without the voice of spiritual consolation, and buried in the deep without the rites of the Church. The food is generally ill selected and seldom sufficiently cooked, in consequence of the insufficiency and bad construction of the cooking places. The supply of water, hardly enough for cooking and drinking, does not allow washing. In many ships the filthy beds, teeming with all abominations, are never required to be brought on deck and aired ; the narrow space between the sleeping berths and the piles of boxes is never washed or scraped, but breathes up a damp and fetid stench, until the day before the arrival at quarantine, when all hands are required to " scrub up," and put on a fair face for the doctor and Government inspector. No moral restraint is attempted, the voice of prayer is never heard ; drunkenness, with its consequent train of ruffianly debasement, is not discouraged, because it is profitable to the captain, who traffics in the grog.

73 Emigrants Suffocated

The scandal of overcrowded ships aroused public horror when the " Londonderry " tragedy became known.

Illustrated London News, 11 December.

The steamer reached the quay of Londonderry with a number of dead bodies on board. In the steerage the dreadful spectacle was exhibited of seventy-three dead bodies piled on each other.

The steamer left Sligo for Liverpool on Friday evening, having on board, besides cattle, nearly 150 passengers, the greater part of whom were on their way to America. The evening became so boisterous that none but the crew could keep the deck, and the passengers were accordingly ordered below. The hatch or companion was drawn across ; but the space for ventilation being insufficient, the unfortunate people below were subjected to the horrible and lingering death of suffocation. One passenger, more fortunate than the rest, succeeded in gaining the deck, and having alarmed the crew, an effort was made for their relief, but too late, 73 human beings having ceased to exist.

It took three hours and a half to get the dead out of the vessel ; and as putrefaction had begun, the smell was so offensive that spirits were given to men to keep them in a state of half-drunkenness to get them to go below. The place in which the poor creatures met their fate was about 20 feet long, 14 feet wide, and 7 feet high. It had

HERE AND THERE ;
Or, Emigration a Remedy.

capacity for about 30 passengers ; but so crowded was it that the dead lay four deep on the floor.

The Promised Land

By contrast with the city slums they had left, to the emigrants the new lands seemed a paradise.

Bradford Observer (quoting an emigrant's letter), 7 December.

Now father, I think this is the Promised Land, but there are faults in it, the water is bad, most of it tastes salt. Adelaide is a very drunken place. Trade is very good here ; they get 7s. a day for plastering. The natives are black. some are almost naked. They get a very good living with begging about Adelaide. We have a beautiful cottage in a gentleman's garden. Wood and water, vegetables and cottage to live in, and I have 20s. a week. I am under gardener. We call it Paradise, for we have all the richest fruits and vegetables that's grown ; we have melons and every sort of pumpkins ; we have the tree of knowledge, peaches, oranges, lemons, grape vines, the tobacco plant. Provisions are very cheap : flour, 2d. per lb. ; mutton, 2d. per lb. ; legs, 3d. per lb. ; beef, 3d. per lb. ; sugar, 3d. and 3½d. per lb. ; best tea, 2s. 6d. per lb. ; tobacco, 3s. for 4 lbs. ; drapery goods are as cheap as in London ; furniture, pots, iron pans, using things are very dear. They think nothing of money here. Ale is 10d. a pot, spirits are very dear, Cape wine is 1s. a bottle. The colony is in a very prosperous state. I often think of my poor father and mother, and brothers and sisters dragged very near to death for half a belly full of meat, while we have plenty of everything and to spare. We ofttimes talk about the poor white slaves of England, the woolcombers, that said they would not transport themselves to the land of full and plenty. I hope you will let the gentlemen read this letter that gave the money to me, to help me to the promised land.

Irish emigrants about to embark for America.

MISCELLANY

Charles Barry's design for the Houses of Parliament was nearing completion.

Pugin was pioneering the Gothic revival. This 1848 dish by him carries a social comment apt to those hungry times.

This was the beginning of the Pre-Raphaelite Brotherhood, started by Rossetti, Millais and Holman Hunt. They painted biblical and literary subjects in a naturalistic style. Below: Millais's Ophelia.

Opposite: Prince Albert introduced a novelty to Britain: the German tradition of Christmas trees.

Illustrated London News.

Illustrated London News, 12 February.

Under the Navigation Laws, certain cargoes reaching Britain had to be carried by British ships with British crews—regardless of how high a tariff the ship-owners charged. When the free-traders sought to have the Laws repealed, there was public outcry. Fearful of foreign competition, seamen marched through London in protest. (The Laws were repealed in 1849.)

Farm Mechanisation Increases

Gardener's Chronicle (Report of the Royal Agricultural Show) 15 July, and Farmer's Herald, January.

One could not help being struck with the increase both in number and amount of certain machines, which but a very few years ago were either wholly unknown, or, at best, very imperfectly understood. Take, for instance, the dibbling machines. Everybody admits the excellence of the practice, but the difficulty was, by mechanical means, to supersede the necessity of relying entirely on such a precarious system as the hand-labour of mere children. The desideratum, if not accomplished, is very nearly so. Again, of draining-tiles : a few years ago, and the very name of a machine for such purpose was unknown. Now they are as plentiful as Blackberries. Just so of long or farm-yard manure drills. Of these we had previously seen and heard of a few attempts at their introduction ; and though we by no means intend to say the implement is perfect, we have no doubt in time it will be so.

Hornsby's Steam-Engine.—Prize £50, at the Royal Agricultural Show of 1848. It took 50 mins. to get up steam and consumed 84lb. coal an hour.

Illustrated London News, 29 July.

Lady's Newspaper, 26 August.
Some domestic innovations that summer :
freezing machine, cooling decanter, siphon,
butter-cooler, wine-cooler.

Cheap Gas

Gradually, private companies were laying
down pipes to bring gas (for lighting only)
to homes and streets.

Illustrated London News, 25 December.

At a meeting of the City Commissioners of
Sewers, a letter was read from the Phoenix
Foundry, Clerkenwell, offering to enter
into a contract for a term of 21 years to
provide the necessary works, main pipes,
and supply the City with gas of the purest
and best quality at 3s. 6d. per thousand
cubic feet.

High-Speed Steam

The new steamships were reducing the
wearisome Atlantic crossing by weeks.

Mining Journal, Railway and Commercial
Gazette, 23 September.

Every succeeding trial proves the great
superiority of British over American
steam-vessels. The British North American
Royal Mail steam-ship, *Niagara*, which
sailed hence on the 19th ult., reached New
York in 12 days and 9 hours. The
American steamer, *Washington*, which
sailed from Cowes on the 20th ult., was
only telegraphed off New York on the 6th
inst., having been 17 days at sea—the
Niagara thus beating her five days, not
taking into account the detention at
Halifax.

The record-breaking " Niagara ": 12 days
to cross the Atlantic.

Dreadful Crimes

Six 19th-century broadside ballads of murders and other crimes, printed in facsimile.

For four centuries, broadside ballads were the newspapers of the nation's poor people. Printed on one side of a sheet and often decorated with a crude woodcut, they were the forerunners of modern cheap newspapers.

We offer facsimile reprints of a set of six ballads, reproduced from the originals and introduced by their owner Leslie Shepard.

Jack Sheppard's Garland
'flash' songs in criminal slang.

Execution of the Five Pirates at Newgate, on Monday, Feb. 22nd 1864 for murder on Board the 'Flowery Land'
mutiny and murder by five sailors on board the vessel 'Flowery Land'.

Murder of M. Marten, by W. Corder/ Wilt Thou Say Farewell Love
a famous murder of 1827, perpetuated ever since in melodramas. Backed with a makeweight simple love song.

Palmer the Poisoner/The Swiss Boy
the story of William Palmer, medical student, racing-man, and coldblooded poisoner, hanged in 1856. With an unrelated fill-up song on the sheet.

Crim. Con, or the Policeman & Bricklayer
the diverting story of how PC. 89 fell for a bricklayer's wife. 'Crim. Con.' was the old term for adultery cases brought by a wronged husband.

We'll not forget Poor Roger Now
the regrettable end of a Claimant who came up the hard way.

The News in Verse

Send 55p (50p plus 5p post and packing) to THEN, 28 James St., Covent Garden, London WC2E 8PA.